Cross Stitch
Floral Designs

Cross Stitch
Floral Designs

Joanne Sanderson

GUILD OF MASTER CRAFTSMAN PUBLICATIONS LTD

First published 2003 by
Guild of Master Craftsman Publications Ltd,
166 High Street, Lewes,
East Sussex, BN7 1XN

ISBN 1 86108 298 3

Cover and book design by Ian Hunt Design
Finished project photography by Christine Richardson
Stitch illustrations by John Yates
Materials courtesy of DMC Creative World Ltd

Picture Acknowledgements
Fitzwilliam Museum, University of Cambridge, UK/
Bridgeman Art Library, page 2
Harry Smith Horticultural Photographic Collection, pages vi, viii, 3–4,
23, 38–39, 63, 64–65, 89, 94–95, 119, 123, endpapers

Typeface: Stempel Schneidler and Stone Sans

Colour origination by Viscan Graphics (Singapore)

Printed and bound in Hong Kong by CT Printing Ltd

I would like to
dedicate this book to

Rianna

as promised.

Contents

Autumn

Winter

Appendix

Introduction

'*Flowers have a language of their own, and it is this bright particular language that we would teach our readers.*'

For as long as I can remember I have loved to see flowers growing in the countryside, in hedges or gracing our gardens. With the projects in this book I have tried to capture the simplicity and beauty of the most popular and best-loved flowers, many of which can be found in my own garden or in the countryside nearby.

The symbolic meaning of flowers dates back to the Elizabethan period, but it was the Victorians who actually assigned simple messages to individual flowers. Flower language became very popular throughout Europe. The first flower dictionary was written by Madame Charlotte de la Tour in 1818 and was entitled *Le Language des Fleurs*. The Victorians were sentimental about flowers and, inspired by this volume, a Miss Corruthers of Inverness wrote her own version in 1879, which has become the standard text on the subject. Society ladies became very familiar with this floral code. And posies were often given by young gentlemen to their sweethearts using the meanings to deliver a secret message.

Each of the four seasonal project chapters is based on the plants of the seasons. I have included a little information about each flower, including, where applicable, its meaning in the 'language of flowers'.

Many countries use flowers as emblems: for example, the English rose, the Welsh daffodil, the Scottish thistle and the Irish shamrock. In Australia, it is the wattle, and Egypt and India share the lotus as their national symbol. Some flowers carry special religious meanings, too.

For me, flowers provide the perfect inspiration for cross stitch designs. Because of its three-dimensional nature, cross stitch is a great medium for producing realistic floral items. It can be created by anyone who can master a few basic stitches. All of which makes floral designs among the most popular of all cross stitch designs.

My early ventures into the garden were the beginning of what has become an enduring passion for plants of all kinds.

A border of mixed flowers with an inscribed message by Joseph Banks, 1814 (watercolour on paper). This delightful card would have accompanied a tailor-made bouquet of flowers to send a special message.

Cross stitch has been a popular pastime since medieval times when clothes began to be decorated with embroidery. In Victorian times, young girls stitched samplers of such skill and beauty that they are very collectable and much sought-after today. The designs in this book are simple, using mainly whole cross stitches and, in some, a little backstitch, making them relatively easy to create. Based on simple botanical illustrations, the designs are varied to cater for both the beginner and more advanced stitcher.

I have stitched the designs on a variety of fabrics, but don't feel limited by my suggestions; let your imagination soar. Try different-coloured fabrics or ways to mount your finished work. If, for instance, you like the white rose cushion design but would prefer it as a picture, just mount it in a suitable square frame instead. Some of the small picture projects could be stitched as cards. The red rose flower-head could be stitched and finished as a coaster or card instead of a trinket pot. The list is endless. And be adventurous; change the colour of a flower to match your decor. If a flower contains three shades of a colour, substitute three shades – dark, medium and light – of an alternative colour. Cross stitch should be enjoyable, so try not to worry too much about technique. Once the humble cross stitch has been mastered, there are no limits to the designs you can stitch. All you need to do is count carefully.

It has been a pleasure designing and stitching these seasonal floral tributes, and I hope that this book will also provide you with many hours of enjoyment, too.

Essentials

Materials and
Equipment 6

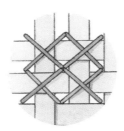

Basic Techniques 8

Materials and Equipment

You only need basic items of material and equipment, much of which is personal preference, to produce stunning cross stitch designs.

Hoops or frames

Whether you use a hoop or scroll frame is down to personal preference, but either one will keep the fabric taut and therefore help you achieve neat stitches with an even tension. By mounting the hoop or scroll frame in a stand you have both hands free. I always use a stand when stitching with a hoop as I can stitch much faster. It is always a good idea to try different methods and see which you prefer. For small projects it may be preferable to simply hold the fabric in your hand while you stitch. A good tip is to spray the fabric you are using with a type of starch used for ironing, then press the fabric to remove the creases. This activates the starch so that the fabric is nice and stiff. If you use a frame or hoop, always make sure it is big enough to cover the whole design when stitched, and remove your work from the hoop when not stitching, as this will help prevent nasty, stubborn creases from forming.

Fabric

There are two main types of fabric used in cross stitch, the main one being Aida 14-count. Aida has 14 x 14 holes per inch (2.5cm), or *hpi*, and is the most widely used fabric. Stitches are made across one block of the fabric. The other fabric is evenweave, for example: linen. The most common evenweave fabric is 28-count which, when worked over two threads, gives the same-sized stitches and appearance as 14-count Aida. The designs in this book are stitched mainly on these two fabrics, so either could be used for each project depending on preference. Beginners may find it easier to stitch on Aida first and try other fabrics later on.

To work out the size of a finished design, divide the stitch count by the fabric count (holes per inch). For example, to find out how large a design 28 x 42 stitches would be on 14-count fabric, divide 28 by 14, which equals 2, and 42 by 14, which equals 3. The finished design would be 2 x 3in (5 x 7.6cm). Always remember to allow an excess for framing of at least 2in (5cm) on each of the four sides when working out how much fabric to use.

Threads

The designs in this book were stitched using DMC six-stranded cotton thread, which comes in 8m skeins. In the United States it is often called floss. Cut the thread to workable lengths, no longer than 18in (45cm) or they will tangle and knot during stitching. Separate all six strands and recombine the number stated in the key; two strands is normally enough as this gives a reasonable coverage with a 14-count fabric. For backstitch, one strand is appropriate to achieve a subtle outline. As you work, let go of the needle from time to time and allow the thread to drop down and unravel itself to help prevent knots forming. If a knot forms, insert the needle into the knot, work the knot loose and gently pull the thread.

Thread sorter

This is a piece of card with holes punched down one side. I recommend you use one of these for large projects, especially when there are several similar colours. Loop each colour onto the card, remembering to write the thread number and symbol from the key alongside it. I always make my own from scraps of card, but you can buy them from most craft shops.

Needles

Stitch the designs with blunt-ended tapestry needles, as these are designed to go through the holes in the fabric easily without piercing or distorting it. I recommend a size 26 for most of the designs stitched in this book. You can buy gold-plated needles which last a lot longer than ordinary nickel-plated ones. They cost a little more, but are a joy to use and ideal for people who have nickel allergies.

Never leave needles in the fabric when you are not actually stitching; over a period of time they may mark the fabric.

Scissors

You need a pair of small, sharp embroidery scissors for snipping threads, and a pair of dressmaking scissors for cutting fabric. Never use these scissors for cutting anything else, such as paper, as this will blunt the scissors.

A selection of materials and equipment for creating the cross stitch designs in this book.

Basic Techniques

This section outlines the basic techniques you need to complete the projects listed in this book.

Preparation

Before you begin, please note that each square on the chart represents a block of fabric or stitch; the solid lines are backstitch. Each symbol represents a cross stitch. The thread colour is shown in the key. French knots are also indicated by symbols in the key.

Method

1. Start in the centre of the design and work outwards unless otherwise stated. To find the centre of the fabric, fold the fabric in half and in half again, then unfold to reveal the centre where the lines intersect.

2. The centre of the chart can be found by aligning the two arrows. The point where the rows meet is the centre point.

3. Identify each colour with the symbol in the key. I recommend that you use a thread sorter and write the symbol for each colour at the side of the relevant thread along with its DMC reference, as some shades of thread are almost identical. Each length of thread is made up of six strands, which you must separate before stitching. Recombine the number of threads in the chosen colour as stated in the key.

4. Start by tying a knot at one end of the thread. Push the needle through the front of the fabric to the back a few stitches away from where you need to start, leaving the knot on the front. Stitch towards the knot and, once you reach it and the stitches are secure, snip it off. To finish, push the needle through to the back of the fabric and weave the thread through several stitches before snipping off neatly. Never start or finish with a knot at the back of the work, as it can show through to the front. Don't be too concerned with the neatness of the back of the work; this can make stitching more of a chore than an enjoyment.

5. Work all cross stitches before completing any backstitch or French knots.

6. Always use an even tension, preferably with a frame or hoop.

7. All top crosses should lie in the same direction. Do not carry long threads across the back from one area to another, as this will affect the tension and they might show. Do not use knots, as they have a nasty habit of working their way to the front of the fabric.

8. Always make sure that your hands are clean and, between stitching, keep work in a bag so that it remains blemish-free. Do not leave needles in the fabric, especially nickel-plated ones; with time these can rust and stain the fabric.

Stitch techniques

Cross stitch

Cross stitches are the main stitch used in this book. They are indicated on the chart by a symbol, each one representing a single cross stitch in the colour indicated by the key at the side of the chart. Unless otherwise stated, always start a design at the centre of the fabric corresponding to the centre of the chart, and work outwards. A cross stitch is worked in two stages over one block on Aida fabric, or over two threads of evenweave fabric. A diagonal stitch is worked first, and then a diagonal stitch in the opposite direction over the first to form a cross (a).

a

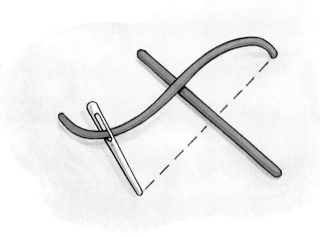

b

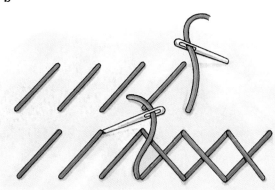

It doesn't matter which way you start the diagonal, i.e. from bottom left to top right or bottom right to top left, but it is important to stick to one or the other so that all top diagonals lie in the same direction to produce a neat professional finish. I recommend that you complete each stitch as you go along but, for larger areas, you may prefer to work in rows. Complete a row of diagonals (the first half of the stitch) and then return along the row stitching the second part of the stitch, the diagonal in the opposite direction (b). When using evenweave fabric, make the stitch over two threads of fabric. When using Aida, make the stitches over one block of fabric.

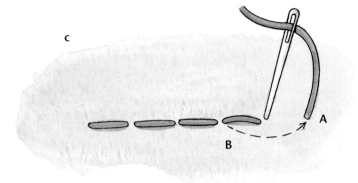

c

Backstitch

This is indicated by a solid line on the chart and is usually worked in one strand of thread. Bring the needle up through the fabric at A and down at B to produce short running stitches (c). Again, when working on evenweave fabrics, make the backstitches over two threads of fabric, and with Aida over one block. Backstitch usually follows the cross stitches, but in some cases the lines on the chart do not. These are long stitches and are worked in exactly the same way as backstitch but, as the name suggests, each stitch is usually longer than one stitch.

French knots

These are used on a few of the designs. Bring the needle up through the fabric as shown, hold the fabric taut and wind it around the needle twice. Push the needle back up through the fabric slightly to the side of where you brought it up. While still holding the thread taut, take the needle all the way through the back of the fabric. As the thread wraps around the needle, a knot is formed (d). A clever alternative to making a French knot is to replace the stitching with seed beads of the same colour.

Three-quarter cross stitch

This is used to lend a smoother outline to a design, and is shown on the chart where a symbol occupies half of a square. To work a three-quarter stitch, work the first half of the cross stitch, i.e. the first diagonal line, but instead of completing the second diagonal, bring the needle up as usual in the opposite corner and then bring it down in the centre. The direction in which the stitch lies is indicated by where the symbol is placed on the chart. If two symbols occupy the same box on the chart, then two of these stitches are completed in the threads indicated by the key. Work the first three-quarter stitch, then using the second colour, complete the stitch to make a whole cross stitch (e).

Finishing

To finish, the embroidery can be washed and ironed. Follow the manufacturer's instructions provided with the threads and fabric used. Use warm water and a mild detergent. If the colours bleed, keep rinsing under warm water until the water runs clear.

d

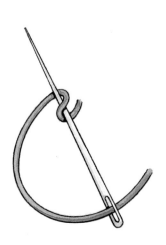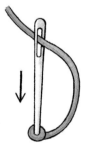

e

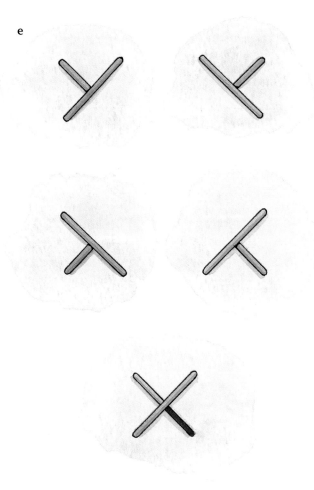

Dry the fabric between the fold of a fluffy white towel and iron on a fairly hot setting. Use cooler settings if metallic thread is used.

Framing

Small pictures can be framed easily without having to take your work to a professional picture framer. Consider whether you require a mount before choosing the frame size, as this may mean you need a bigger frame. Cut a piece of cardboard the same size as the back of the frame. Attach double-sided tape along all four sides and fold the finished fabric with the wrong sides facing around the board, making sure that the picture is centred. Wadding can be used if you need it, placed between the fabric and board. To secure everything, tape the edges of the fabric to the board using masking tape before placing in the frame. Choosing acid-free materials ensures

that your stitching will be preserved for a long time. Decide if the glass you are going to use is ordinary glass or non-reflective glass. Non-reflective glass is the best choice in a room that is well-lit, or if it is going to be displayed near a window. After sandwiching the finished work between the glass and backing board, seal the frame with gummed brown paper (the kind used for parcels) to protect against moisture and dust. If you plan to hang the picture in a bathroom, seal with silicone sealant instead of gummed, brown paper. Never hang your framed work opposite a window; strong sunlight will bleach the colour of the materials. Before you stitch, it is important to allow enough extra fabric for an extra 3 or 4in (7.5 or 10cm) on a medium-sized design. It will also mean that you are not limited to using a particular frame size, too.

Mounting a card

Choose a three-fold card mount with an aperture of a suitable size and shape. To see which colour card best complements your work, lay your piece against several colours, taking into consideration the various colours used in the design. Stick double-sided tape around the aperture of the card on the wrong side. Lay your work face up. Place the card with the aperture centrally over your stitching and press into place; the tape will hold it secure. Trim the fabric if necessary to fit the card. Place the card and stitching face down and stick the left-hand third over the fabric using double-sided tape. The card should open correctly.

Other methods of presentation

The designs in this book could be presented in several ways depending on your choice and the size of the finished design. There is a good range of products available, including trinket pots, coasters and paperweights. Follow the manufacturer's instructions when using these. See the suppliers listed at the back of the book (see page 126) for a range of suppliers of different products.

Spring

'When youthful spring around us breathes,
Thy spirit warms her fragrant sigh,
And every flower the summer wreathes
Is born beneath that kindling eye:
Where're we turn Thy glories shine,
And all things fair and bright are Thine.'

(Thomas Moore)

Spring is a time of rebirth and optimism. As the first green shoots appear, the days become longer, promising sunshine and brighter days on the way.

For me, the sight of the magnolia bloom has to be one of the most beautiful. The fresh bright colours of the daffodil and tulip, for me, radiate sunshine. If you are a beginner, try stitching the smaller designs. The viola, bluebell and primula are delicate tributes to the new season, and the wake-robin coaster will make a lovely gift or keepsake. This is the first coaster design of four, one for each season. For a complete set, why not make them all.

Magnolia Set

The magnolia tree is one of the first to blossom in spring, although some species do flower later, in early summer. The beautiful, creamy, blush-tinted flowers have a wonderful scent. Most varieties bloom well before the tree is laden with leaves.

Originating in the East, one of the first magnolia species to arrive in England, *Magnolia wilsonii,* was brought from China in 1904 by plant collector Ernest Henry Wilson, and was then named after him. He was responsible for introducing many different plant species from the East to Europe, and specimens were displayed in Kew gardens in London.

It is one of the most beautiful spring-flowering trees and, while the blooms are short-lived, they are a must for every garden.

There is no backstitch used in these designs. I have taken one of the magnolia blooms from the picture and stitched and mounted it for display in a trinket pot, but you can also mount it in a card or coaster, if you prefer.

VICTORIAN LANGUAGE
OF FLOWERS

The magnolia means magnificence and strength.

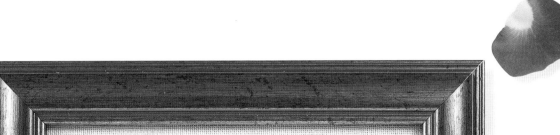

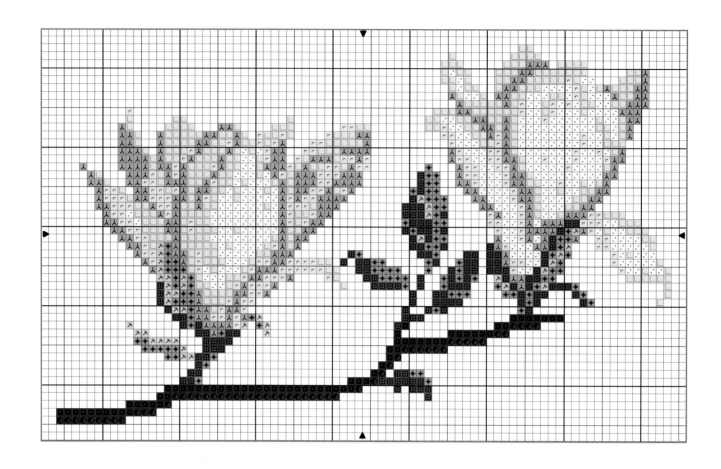

Magnolia picture

Materials

- 28-count white Brittney (Zweigart 100), 10 x 12in (25.5 x 30.5cm)
- DMC stranded cotton as listed in the key
- Size 26 tapestry needle
- Frame with an aperture 5 x 7in (12.5 x 18cm)

Design size

5¾ x 3⅜in (14.5 x 8.7cm) at 14-count

Stitch count

80 x 48

Thread key

		DMC
+	Pistachio Green Medium	368
⊞	Pistachio Green Dark	367
↗	Pistachio Green Light	369
◑	Brown Dark	3781
	Flesh Light	3770
⋅	Winter White	3865
◼	Brown Medium	3790
r	Peach Light	948
人	Flesh Medium	950

Note: use two strands for cross stitch

Magnolia ceramic bowl

Materials

- 14-count white Aida 6in (15.3cm) square
- DMC stranded cotton as listed in the key
- Size 26 tapestry needle
- Framecraft ivory ceramic bowl (PL5: 8.9cm)

Design size

3in (7.6cm) square at 14-count

Stitch count

42 x 42

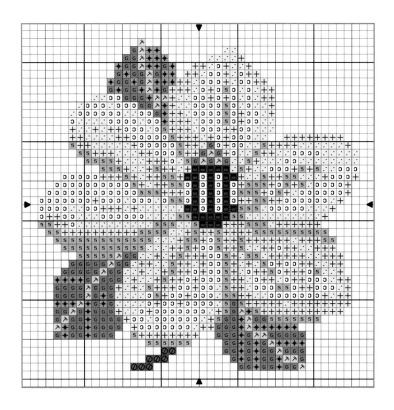

Thread key	DMC
Flesh Light	3770
Winter White	3865
Flesh Medium	950
Pistachio Green Dark	367
Peach Light	948
Pistachio Green Medium	368
Pistachio Green Light	369
Terracotta Dark	355
Brown Medium	3790

Note: use two strands for cross stitch

Magnolia trinket pot

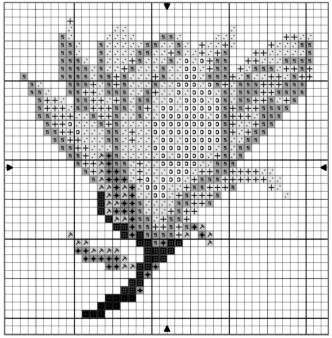

Materials

- 18-count white Aida, 6in (15.3cm) square
- DMC stranded cotton as listed in the key
- Size 26 tapestry needle
- Framecraft ivory trinket pot (PL3: 6.5cm)
- Iron-on interfacing, e.g. Vilene (optional)

Design size

2in (5cm) square at 18-count

Stitch count

38 x 38

Method

1 Stitch all the designs in the same way. Find the centre of the fabric and begin stitching here, following the chart. Work the cross stitches over two threads of fabric for the picture on evenweave fabric, and over one block on Aida for the two smaller designs.

2 Work two strands of thread for cross stitch as indicated in the key.

3 Once you have completed the stitching, press the fabric and mount following the manufacturer's instructions. For framing techniques, see page 11.

4 I recommend that you use lightweight iron-on interfacing or Vilene to back the work and prevent it from fraying.

5 Cut out the design to fit the ceramic bowl and trinket pot, using the acetate disc provided with the kit as a template. Position the acetate centrally over the stitching and draw around it with a pencil, then cut out carefully, following the pencil line. Assemble according to the manufacturer's instructions.

Thread key		DMC
+	Peach Light	948
✚	Pistachio Green Medium	368
▦	Pistachio Green Dark	367
⋱	Flesh Light	3770
5	Flesh Medium	950
⤜	Pistachio Green Light	369
ↄ	Winter White	3865
▨	Brown Medium	3790

Note: use two strands for cross stitch

Tulip and Daffodil Pictures

The tulip is thought to have originated in the Middle East where the name comes from the Turkish word 'tulband' meaning 'turban' which refers to the shape of the flowers.

In the last few hundred years, tulips have been associated with the Netherlands where they are grown in their masses, a truly spectacular sight. In the 1600s, some tulip bulbs were so highly prized that a bride's dowry could be bought with them. Promissory notes were exchanged instead of cash which, at the time, caused the collapse of the bulb market in Holland. In the nineteenth century, bulb flowers became more accessible because of their low prices. Today, the market thrives; the tulip is easily affordable and is enjoyed in gardens worldwide. It has even become the national symbol of the Netherlands.

The daffodil is of the genus narcissus, which includes varieties with long and short trumpets. Species of wild daffodils are native to England

VICTORIAN LANGUAGE
OF FLOWERS

The tulip is a symbol of love. A red tulip represents a declaration of love and a yellow tulip means a refusal.

The daffodil is often associated with chivalry.

and Wales where they thrive in woodland habitats. It is the national flower of Wales and also the flower of St David, its patron saint. This is most likely because it blooms around the same time as St David's day, which is 1st of March. It is traditional to give daffodils as a present on Mothering Sunday and to display picked daffodils at Easter, too.

This pretty pair of pictures will bring the freshness of spring to any room. They are stitched on 28-count white fabric, but can also be stitched on 14-count Aida to the same size. The designs are relatively simple to stitch, and include a small amount of backstitch.

Materials
For each picture:
- 28-count white Quaker Cloth (Zweigart 100), 10 x 12 in (25 x 30cm)
- DMC stranded cotton as listed in the key
- Size 26 tapestry needle
- Frame with an aperture 10 x 8in (25 x 30cm) and a mount with an aperture 5 x 7in (12.5 x 18cm)

Daffodil

Design size
3⅜ x 6⅛in (8.7 x 15.8cm) at 14-count

Stitch count
48 x 86

Tulip

Design size
3⅛ x 6⅛in (8 x 15.6cm) at 14-count

Stitch count
44 x 86

Method

1 Stitch both designs in the same way. Find the centre of the fabric and begin here, following the chart. Work the cross stitches over two threads of fabric. For instructions on how to make a cross stitch, please see page 8.

2 Work the design using two strands of thread for cross stitch and one for backstitch as indicated in the key.

3 Once the stitching is complete, press the fabric and mount in your chosen frame. For tips on framing, please refer to page 11.

Thread key

		DMC				DMC
+	Pistachio Green Light	368	×	Yellow Light	745
□	Pistachio Green Medium	320	2	Yellow	727
■	Green	986	+	Yellow Medium	743
↖	Green Light	3348	↙	Orange Yellow	742
○	Brown Light	3045	S	Orange	740

Backstitch

		DMC
▬▬	Orange Yellow	742
▬▬	Orange	740

Note: use two strands for cross stitch
and one for backstitch

Thread key

		DMC				DMC
⬜	Pistachio Green Medium	320	✚	Yellow Medium		743
✚	Pistachio Green Light	368	∩	Orange		972
♥	Green Light	989	▦	Pistachio Green Dark		367
✕	Yellow Light	745				

Backstitch

		DMC
▬	Orange	972
▬	Pistachio Green Dark	367

Note: use two strands for cross stitch and one for backstitch

Wake-robin Coaster

The wake-robin is of the genus trillium, which means 'trinity flower', probably because it has three petals, symbolizing the Holy Trinity. The wake-robin is also commonly known as the wood lily, as it thrives in shady woodland areas and rich, moist soil. It flowers primarily in spring, although some species flower in autumn. The blooms are usually white but turn a delicate pink with age. This beautiful plant looks exotic in any setting.

This simple design has been mounted in a coaster. Requiring only a few colour threads and a little backstitch, it is perfect for the beginner. I have stitched the wake-robin onto a cream evenweave fabric, but you can use Aida if you prefer. Lay the threads across a selection of different-coloured fabrics to see which combination you like best.

Materials

- 28-count cream Quaker cloth (Zweigart 222), 6in (15.3cm)
- DMC stranded cotton as listed in the key
- Size 26 tapestry needle
- Framecraft coaster
- Iron-on interfacing, e.g. Vilene (optional)

Design size

2⅜ x 2¼in (6.3 x 5.7cm) at 14-count

Stitch count

34 x 31

Method

1 Find the centre of the fabric and begin stitching from here, following the chart. Work the cross stitches over two threads of fabric.
2 Use two strands of thread for cross stitch, and one for backstitch and French knots as indicated in the key.
3 Once you have completed the stitching, press the fabric and mount in the coaster following the manufacturer's instructions. I recommend that you use lightweight iron-on interfacing or Vilene to back the work and prevent fraying.
4 Cut out the design to fit the coaster.

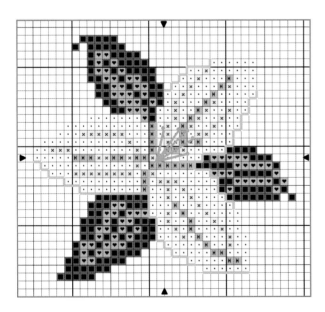

Thread key

		DMC
♥	Green Light	989
■	Green Dark	986
·	White Bright	B5200
✕	Grey Light	762
Ħ	Grey	415

Backstitch

	Orange	972
	Grey	415

French knots

●	Orange	972

Note: use two strands for cross stitch and one for backstitch and French knots.

Camellia Card
and Coaster

A beautiful evergreen shrub, the camellia's gorgeous roselike blooms come in an abundance of glorious colours. The camellia favours a slightly warmer climate and does not respond well to frost. Most varieties flower in spring, but some flower as late as autumn and winter.

The camellia combines the fresh beauty of an early rose but, as an evergreen, provides yearlong interest to the garden.

I have chosen a pink variety for this small, simple card, and stitched it onto a matching fabric. I have also stitched the camellia onto white fabric and mounted it in a coaster using the same chart. This is to demonstrate the different effects you can achieve by changing the colour of the fabric. I have stitched both designs using an evenweave fabric, but you could use 14-count Aida to attain the same size. There is no backstitch used in this design.

Camellia card

Materials

- 28-count baby pink Cashel linen (Zweigart 402), 6in (15.3cm) square
- DMC stranded cotton as listed in the key
- Size 26 tapestry needle
- Three-fold card with a 4in (10cm) circular aperture

Design size

2⅝in (6.5cm) square at 14-count

Stitch count

36 x 37

Camellia coaster

Materials

- 28-count white Quaker cloth (Zweigart 100), 6in (15.3cm) square
- DMC stranded cotton as listed in the key
- Size 26 tapestry needle
- Fabric Flair square coaster

Design size

2⅝in (6.5cm) square at 14-count

Stitch count

36 x 37

Method

1 Stitch both the card and coaster in the same way, following the same chart. Find the centre of the fabric and begin stitching. You may find it easier to stitch the darker shades of pink first, before filling in with the paler shades. Work the cross stitches over two threads of fabric.

2 Use two strands of thread for cross stitch as indicated in the key.

3 Once you have completed the stitching, press the fabric and mount in the card aperture or coaster following the manufacturer's instructions.

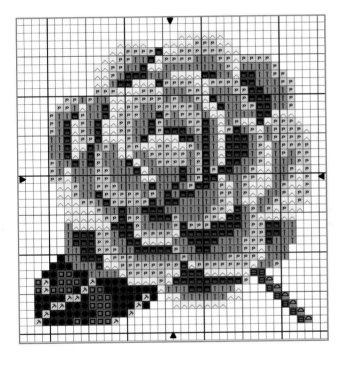

Thread key		DMC
⋀	Pink Very Light	819
p	Rose	963
↑	Rose Medium	962
▮	Rose Dark	3350
●	Green Very Dark	500
⤬	Pistachio Green Light	369
▣	Green Medium	987
▤	Cocoa Dark	779
⌂	Cocoa Light	3861

Note: use two strands for cross stitch

Fritillary Hobby Box

Majestic in any border with its bright clusters of orange bell-shaped flowers, *Fritillaria imperialis* is more commonly known as crown imperial, and in Europe as the Easter lily. A stunning spring-flowering bulb, it is a firm cottage garden favourite where it mixes well with other cottage garden plants. I think it looks particularly striking partnered with tulips and daffodils. In bright sunshine and well-drained soil, it can grow to a height of over 3ft (1m). The snake's head fritillary (*Fritallaria meleagris*) is a very popular specimen but much smaller at just 12in (30cm) in height. Its name is a reference to its pretty check-patterned petals.

The fritillary has been mounted in a box lid, but could be framed to match the daffodil and tulip designs. Again, I have chosen a white 28-count fabric, but it could also be stitched using 14-count Aida to the same size.

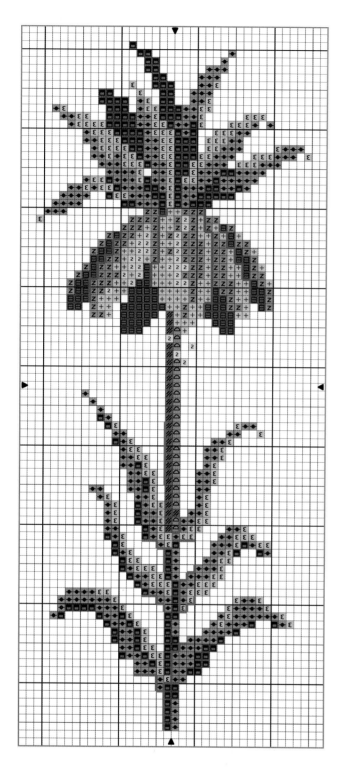

Materials

- 28-count white Quaker Cloth (Zweigart 100), 10 x 12in (25 x 30cm)
- DMC stranded cotton as listed in the key
- Size 26 tapestry needle
- Framecraft hobby box (WHB1)

Design size

2⅝ x 6¼in (6.5 x 15.8cm) at 14-count

Stitch count

36 x 87

Method

1 Find the centre of the fabric and begin stitching from here, following the chart. Work the cross stitches over two threads of fabric.

2 Use two strands of thread for cross stitch and one for backstitch as indicated in the key.

3 Once you have completed the stitching, press the fabric and mount in your chosen box lid following the manufacturer's instructions. You can, if you wish, sandwich wadding between the fabric and backing board for a better fit.

Thread key	DMC
Green Dark	904
Green	470
Green Light	472
Cocoa Dark	451
Yellow Medium	743
Orange	741
Orange Red	900
Cocoa Light	3861
Yellow Light	727

Backstitch

Green Dark	904
Orange Red	900

Note: use two strands for cross stitch and one for backstitch

Iris Noteblock

The iris is associated with February and May. There are many varieties of this flower, in multitudinous shades of blue and purple. I have chosen *Iris reticulata*, a miniature bulb, which makes a stunning display. As spring dawns, it is always a joy to behold the first appearance of this unusually shaped flower in my garden.

This design is stitched on 14-count white Aida, but you could use a 28-count evenweave and stitch over two threads of fabric.

The design is mostly made up of cross stitches but there is a small amount of backstitch, too. I have mounted the iris in a noteblock, but you could use a card, small frame or even a square coaster to display it.

Materials

- 14-count white Aida 6in (15.3cm)
- DMC stranded cotton as listed in the key
- Size 26 tapestry needle
- Framecraft noteblock (CNB)
- Iron-on interfacing, e.g. Vilene (optional)
- Fray Check (optional)

Design size

2¾ x 3⅛in (7 x 7.7cm) at 14-count

Stitch count

38 x 44

Method

1 Find the centre of the fabric and start here following the chart. Work the cross stitches over one block of fabric.

2 Use two strands of thread for cross stitch and one for backstitch as indicated in the key.

3 Once you have completed all the stitching, press the fabric and mount in the noteblock following the manufacturer's instructions. I recommend that you mount the fabric onto Vilene before cutting it out, then seal the edges with Fray Check to prevent fraying. Finally, mount the design into the noteblock.

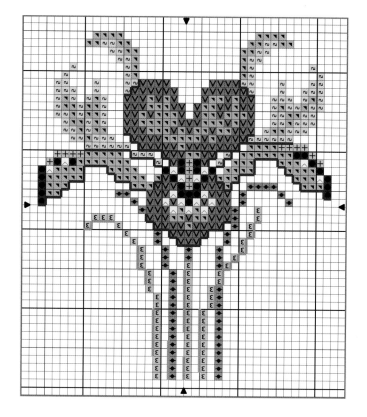

Thread key

		DMC
+	Yellow	726
ε	Green Pale	472
V	Blue Violet Medium	340
■	Blue Violet Dark	333
◣	Blue Violet	341
∼	Blue Violet Light	3747
◆	Green	470
∧	White	BLANC

Backstitch

▬	Blue Violet Dark	333
▬	Green	470

Note: use two strands for cross stitch and one for backstitch

Primula, Viola and Bluebell Set

There are many species of primula, including primroses and cowslips. The primrose is found in woodland areas throughout Europe and the cowslip is found in Europe and Asia. The latter should not be confused with the American cowslip, which is a different plant altogether.

The viola favours the world's temperate regions. The 500 or more species of viola all share the same characteristic of having five petals. Violas belong to the same family as the pansy and are, in fact, the ancestors of the modern pansy. The viola is associated with the month of November and, mounted in a card, would make a delightful greeting for someone with a birthday at this time.

Bluebells can be found in British woodland areas, where the thick blue carpet of flowers is a breathtaking sight. For some reason, these days, the bluebell is sadly declining in numbers and we can only speculate as to why; perhaps because of woodland management.

The Elizabethans used the ground bulbs of bluebells to form a paste, which they used to stiffen their ruffs – the fashionable collar of the day – and in bookbinding, too.

These designs are very simple to stitch, and can be mounted in cards or small frames. I have stitched them onto an evenweave fabric, but you could use 14-count Aida, or change the colour of the fabric, if you prefer.

Primula notebook

Materials

- 28-count white Quaker cloth (Zweigart 100), 6½ x 8½in (16.5 x 21.6cm)
- DMC stranded cotton as listed in the key
- Size 26 tapestry needle
- Framecraft notebook (BA5)

Design size

1¾ x 3⅝in (4.3 x 9.3cm) at 14-count

Stitch count

24 x 51

Viola picture

Materials

- 28-count baby blue Cashel linen (Zweigart 562), 6 x 7in (15 x 17.5cm)
- DMC stranded cotton as listed in the key
- Size 26 tapestry needle
- A small brass effect frame with an aperture 3 x 4in (7.5 x 10cm)
- Ribbon (optional)

Design size

2⅛ x 3½in (5.4 x 8.9cm) at 14-count

Stitch count

30 x 49

Bluebell notelet

Materials

- 28-count Forget-me-knot blue Jobelan (Fabric Flair) 6 x 8in (15 x 20cm)
- DMC stranded cotton as listed in the key
- Size 26 tapestry needle
- Craft Creations card blank, 4 x 6in (10 x 15cm) with an oval aperture

Design size

2 x 4¼in (5 x 10.7cm) at 14-count

Stitch count

28 x 59

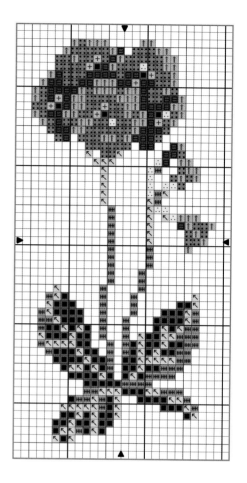

Thread key		DMC
↑	Pink Light	605
	Pink Medium	603
	Pink Dark	601
⊞	Green	988
	Green Dark	986
↖	Green Light	3348
∴	Yellow Light	3823
+	Yellow	726

Note: Use two strands for cross stitch

Method

1 Stitch all the designs in the same way. Find the centre of the fabric and begin stitching from here, following the chart. Work the cross stitches over two strands of fabric.

2 Use two strands of thread for cross stitch and one for backstitch as indicated in the key.

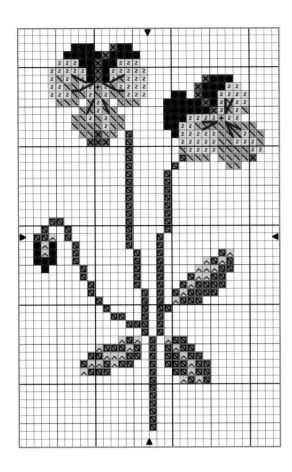

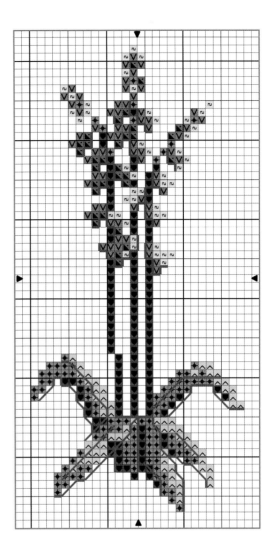

Thread key

		DMC
	Violet Dark	550
	Violet Medium	553
	Green Light	966
	Green Dark	505
	Yellow Green	907
	Yellow Light	727
	Yellow Dark	725

Backstitch

	Violet Dark	550

Note: use two strands for cross stitch
and one for backstitch

Thread key

		DMC
	Blue Violet Medium	340
	Lavender Blue	3838
	Blue Violet Light	3747
	Green Dark	561
	Green Medium	3816
	Green Light	966

Backstitch

	Green Dark	561
	Blue Violet Dark	333

Note: use two strands for cross stitch

3 Once you have completed the stitching, press the fabric and mount following the manufacturer's instructions. For tips on mounting cards, see page 11. For the notebook, use the same technique as for mounting a card. You can frame the card in its mount using a 6 x 8in (15 x 20cm) frame.

Summer

'Now summer is in flower, and nature's hum
Is never silent round her bounteous bloom;
Insects, as small as dust, have never done
With glittering dance, and reeling in the sun;
And green wood fly, and blossom haunting bee
Are never weary of their melody.'

(John Clare)

Summer evokes idyllic images of cottage gardens and
scented blooms, old-fashioned roses and bees buzzing
around stems of lavender. Try stitching the rose picture; it
sums up what summer is for me. If you are a beginner, the
sweet pea card or clematis trinket pot are ideal projects to get
you started. The lavender notebook and scented sachet
would make a lovely gift for someone special, and the
rhododendron wall hanging is a cheerful addition to a living
room wall.

Rose Set

The rose is traditionally the queen of flowers. It has been appreciated by people the world over since ancient times for its colour, scent and medicinal properties. The Greeks named the flower and were the first to grow it in their gardens. They also wrote poems about it and painted its likeness on temple walls. Cleopatra was said to have seduced Mark Anthony in a throne room filled knee-deep with rose petals. The Romans also loved the rose so much that they began planting it instead of olive trees. It was the Persians who first crushed the petals to make rose oil.

The rose became popular in England during Tudor times; the Tudor rose combined the red rose of Lancaster and the white rose of York. Elizabeth I adopted the rose as her emblem, a symbol of purity. During the Victorian period, the red rose became a token of love and passion and even today it is still considered a romantic symbol.

The five petals of the wild rose were also supposed to represent the five wounds of Christ.

The rose is the birthday flower for the month of October and sometimes June.

The rose picture contains whole cross stitches and a tiny amount of backstitch, although not in the flower-head. The design is stitched as a crystal bowl, too, but it could also be mounted in a coaster. I have stitched both designs using a white evenweave fabric, but you could use 14-count Aida; the size remains the same.

VICTORIAN LANGUAGE
OF FLOWERS

*The red rose means love
and passion;
a white rose means idealistic
love, discretion and purity;
a pink rose, grace;
a yellow rose, jealousy;
a wild rose, pleasure
and pain.*

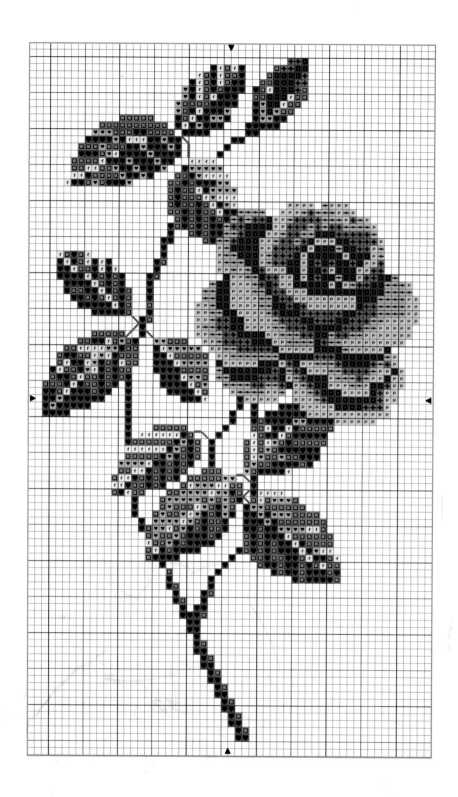

Thread key

		DMC				DMC
▼	Green Dark	895	f	Green Light	772	
▢	Green Medium	987	♥	Green	989	
p	Rose	963	◼	Rose Very Dark	326	
◆	Rose Medium	3716	◆	Rose Dark	335	

Backstitch

▨▨▨ Green Dark 895

Note: use two strands for cross stitch and one for backstitch

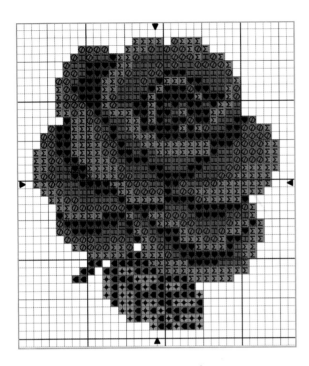

Thread key

		DMC
Σ	Coral	351
◄	Green Dark	561
✦	Green	3816
∅	Red	3801
▼	Red Dark	777
⊥	Red Medium	321

Note: use two strands for cross stitch
and one for backstitch

Red rose crystal bowl

Materials
- 28-count white Brittney (Zweigart 100),
  5in (12.5cm) square
- DMC stranded thread as listed in the key
- Size 26 tapestry needle
- Framecraft crystal bowl (CT3: 6.5cm)

Design size
2¼ x 2⅝in (5.7 x 6.4cm) at 14-count

Stitch count
32 x 37

Method

1 Find the centre of the fabric and begin stitching
  from here following the chart. Work the cross
  stitches over two threads of fabric.

2 Use two strands of thread for cross stitch as
  indicated in the key.

3 Once you have completed the stitching, press
  the fabric and mount in the lid of the crystal bowl
  following the manufacturer's instructions.

4 I recommend that you use lightweight iron-on
  interfacing or Vilene to back the work and
  prevent fraying.

5 Cut out the design to fit the crystal bowl, using
  the acetate disc as a template. Centre the acetate
  over the stitching and draw around it with a
  pencil, then cut out following the pencil line
  carefully. Assemble according to the
  manufacturer's instructions.

Pink rose picture

Materials
- 28-count white Quaker cloth (Zweigart 100),
  10 x 12in (25 x 30cm)
- DMC stranded cotton as listed in the key
- Size 26 tapestry needle
- Frame 10 x 8in (25 x 20cm) and a mount with an
  aperture of 6 x 8in (15 x 20cm)

Design size
3⅞ x 6¾in (10 x 17cm) at 14-count

Stitch count
54 x 95

Method

1 Find the centre of the fabric and start here
  following the chart. Work the cross stitches over
  two threads of fabric.

2 Use two strands of thread for cross stitch and one
  for backstitch as indicated in the key.

3 Once the stitching is complete, press the fabric
  and mount in your chosen frame.

Carnation and Marguerite Pictures

There are thought to be over 300 species of carnation today. In China, one variety is mentioned in texts dating back to AD 23 and others are thought to be older still. The carnation was not introduced into Europe until the 1700s.

The carnation is associated with the month of September and sometimes December. It is often given to say thank you. The sweet william, a variety of carnation, was very popular at that time and represented gallantry. In America, it is worn on Mother's day as a token of respect: a coloured carnation if one's mother is alive, and white if not.

The marguerite is a member of the chrysanthemum family and its Latin name is *Chrysanthemum frutescens*.

Today, many chrysanthemums are grown for decoration, and the marguerite is no exception with its attractive white, pink or yellow daisy-like heads. The marguerite looks particularly effective planted in pots or containers. In a shady corner, the white flowers have an almost transparent quality and, in the evening, remain visible long after the other flowers disappear in the fading light.

The carnation design contains only six colours and includes a little backstitch, making it a simple project to stitch. The marguerite is an elegant yet simple flower, and looks stunning stitched on pink fabric, but it would also be lovely on other pastel shades such as yellow or pale blue.

VICTORIAN LANGUAGE
OF FLOWERS

The carnation means divine love, encouragement and wealth.

Materials

For each picture:

- 28-count white Quaker Cloth (Zweigart 100), 10 x 8in (25 x 20cm)
- 28-count pink Cashel linen (Zweigart 402), 10 x 8in (25 x 20cm) (for the marguerite)
- DMC stranded cotton as listed in the key
- Size 26 tapestry needle
- Frame 6 x 8in (15 x 20cm) with a suitable mount

Carnation

Design size

3⅛ x 5¼in (7.7 x 13.3cm) at 14-count

Stitch count

44 x 74

Marguerite

Design size

3½ x 5¾in (9 x 14.5cm) at 14-count

Stitch count

49 x 81

Method

1 Find the centre of the fabric and begin stitching from here following the chart. Work the cross stitches over two threads of fabric.

2 Use two strands of thread for cross stitch and one for backstitch as indicated in the key.

3 Once you have completed the stitching, press the fabric and mount in your chosen frame.

Thread key — DMC

1	Pink Very Light	818
	Dusty Rose	3716
▲	Dusty Rose Medium	3833
=	Green	563
N	Green Dark	562
✕	Green Light	369

Backstitch

	Dusty Rose Medium	3833

Note: use two strands for cross stitch and one for backstitch

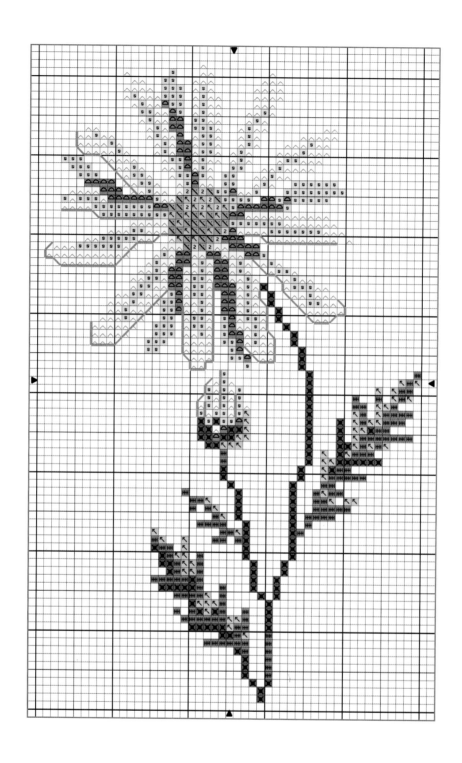

Thread key

		DMC				
∧	White	BLANC	2	Yellow	727	
✕	Green Dark	367	╲	Yellow Dark	725	
⫟	Green	988	s	Grey Light	168	
↖	Green Light	3348	◠	Grey Medium	169	

Backstitch

— Grey Medium 169

Note: use two strands for cross stitch and one for backstitch

Rhododendron Wall Hanging

The lush, glossy, green leaves and abundance of beautiful flowers make the rhododendron an enduringly popular plant. Native to the Sichuan region of China and the Himalayan area of Tibet, the genus rhododendron includes the azalea, and there are both evergreen and deciduous varieties. However, all these species suffer in limey soil.

I have chosen to stitch several varieties together but each could be stitched and framed individually. I have chosen Aida but you may use 28-count evenweave to make the same finished design size. If using even weave fabric, remember to stitch over two threads of fabric.

VICTORIAN LANGUAGE
OF FLOWERS

The rhododendron is often associated with danger or warning. The azalea means moderation.

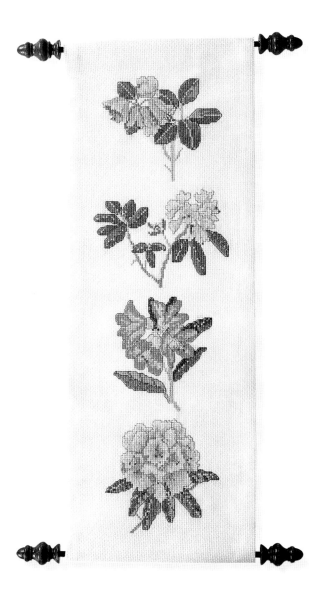

Materials
- 14-count white Aida (Zweigart 100), 11 x 23in (28 x 58cm)
- DMC stranded cotton as listed in the key
- Size 26 tapestry needle
- A hanger or bell-pull 8in (20cm) long
- Backing fabric, 10 x 23in (25 x 58cm)

Design size
5½ x 17¾in (14 x 45cm) at 14-count

Stitch count
77 x 244

Method
1 Find the centre of the fabric and begin stitching from here following the chart. Work the cross stitches over one block of fabric.
2 Use two strands of thread for cross stitch and French knots and one for backstitch as indicated in the key. It might be useful to use a thread sorter here as the shades of colour are quite similar.

Thread key

		DMC
Σ	Dusty Rose Dark	961
ρ	Dusty Rose Light	963
↑	Dusty Rose Medium	962
•→	Dusty Rose	3716
S	Orange	740
∧	Pink Very Light	819
1	Pink Light	818
◼	Pistachio Green Very Dark	319
—	Pistachio Green Very Light	369
I	Pistachio Green Light	368
⊠	Pistachio Green Medium	320
◀	Pistachio Green Dark	367
✛	Light Brown	3046
×	Yellow Light	745
+	Yellow Medium	743
∩	Burnt Orange	972
▦	Tan	436

Backstitch

——	Dusty Rose Dark	961
——	Pistachio Green Very Dark	319
——	Pistachio Green Very Light	369
——	Copper	920
——	Brown	435

French knots

●	Copper	920

Note: use two strands for cross stitch
and one for backstitch

3 Once the stitching is complete, press the fabric.

4 With right sides of the backing fabric and finished work facing, stitch down either side, making the finished piece just under 8in (20cm) in width to allow the bell-pull room to fit. Make sure the design is centred. Press the seams and turn the right way.

5 To neaten, fold the bottom and top edges over about 1in (2.5cm) and slip stitch to secure. Remove one end of each bell-pull and thread through the top and bottom edges.

Poppy Cushion Cover

Poppies have a long and fascinating history; garlands of the flower have been found in Egyptian tombs dating back to the Pharaohs. Drugs such as morphine and opium derive from the poppy (*Papaver somniferum*). Opium is used as an analgesic to reduce pain and is a narcotic, because it induces sleep. For many, however, the poppy is most well-known as a symbol of remembrance for the soldiers who gave their lives in World War I. Poppies

sprung up in the fields in France where so many died, and it is for this reason that the flower is worn on November 11th, Remembrance Day. Perhaps because of this, it has come to mean consolation.

Today, there are over 100 species of poppy in existence. Perhaps the best-loved of all the species is the common field poppy, *Papaver rheos*, which grows in Britain almost like a weed, along roadsides, in hedges and speckled through fields of corn.

This design would suit a more experienced stitcher or one who would like a challenge.

The design includes whole cross stitches and a little backstitch. It is stitched onto evenweave fabric, which makes it stand out. You could stitch it on Aida and mount it in a frame if you prefer. If you do, use 18-count Aida, which will reduce the size slightly. Continue to use two strands of thread for cross stitch to make the poppy really stand out against the Aida.

Thread key

		DMC
◩	Coral Dark	349
✚	Coral Medium	350
⋁	Hunter Green Light	3347
⬓	Hunter Green Dark	3345
◤	Avocado Green Pale	472
Z	Avocado Green	471
◥	Peach Medium	3341
⠿	Peach Dark	3340
▼	Red Dark	304
■	Black	310
✳	Garnet	814

Backstitch

▬	Hunter Green Dark	3345
▬	Peach Medium	3341
▬	Garnet	814

French knots

●	Black	310

Note: use two strands for cross stitch and one for backstitch

Materials

- 28-count white Quaker Cloth, 20in (50cm) square
- DMC stranded cotton as listed in the key
- Size 26 tapestry needle
- Cushion pad 14in (35cm) square
- Two pieces of white backing fabric, each 20 x 11in (50 x 28cm)
- Zip, 10in (25cm) long

Design size

7⅜ x 8¾in (19 x 22cm) at 14-count

Stitch count

103 x 122

Method

1 Find the centre of the fabric and start here following the chart. Work the cross stitches over two threads of fabric.
2 Use two strands of thread for cross stitch and French knots and one for backstitch as indicated in the key. Before you begin, sort your threads onto a thread sorter to avoid confusing the many shades of reds and greens in this design.
3 Once you have completed the stitching, press the fabric.
4 Stitch the two halves of backing fabric together, and insert the zip.
5 With right sides facing, stitch the backing fabric and finished work together.
6 Turn the cushion right side out.
7 Measure and mark a square 14in (35cm) square, ensuring the design is centred. Complete a line of satin stitch around each side of the marked square.
8 Press and insert the cushion pad.

Lavender Notebook and Sachet

A popular herb garden plant, lavender is proven to have antiseptic and analgesic properties. Lavender has a wonderful, unforgettable scent and is used widely in aromatherapy because it encourages relaxation and restful sleep. This evergreen plant makes thick, fragrant hedging and forms neat rows in formal knot gardens.

Both lavender projects would make a lovely, thoughtful gift. Fill the lavender sachet with dried lavender, place it on your pillow or hang it in your wardrobe. For the notebook, stitch the design and mount it into a three-fold card and send it to someone special. Alternatively, mount it in a small frame.

I have used three strands of thread to stitch the flower-heads and two for the stems to make the flowers really stand out authentically. Stitched in whole cross stitch only, and using the same chart for both projects, these pretty designs are ideal for the beginner.

VICTORIAN LANGUAGE
OF FLOWERS

Lavender was sent as a message of refusal but, conversely, it can also represent undying love.

Lavender notebook

Materials

- White Aida band (2in Zweigart E7107), 26 stitches wide and 18in (45cm) long
- DMC stranded cotton as listed in the key
- Size 26 tapestry needle
- A5 pale purple notebook

Design size

1⅝ x 4⅞in (3.8 x 12.1cm) at 14-count

Stitch count

22 x 68

Method

1 Find the centre of the fabric and begin stitching following the chart. Work the cross stitches over one block of fabric.

2 Use two strands of thread for the green shades and three strands for the purple shades as indicated in the key. There is no backstitch in this design.

3 Once you have completed the stitching, press the fabric and wrap the piece around the cover of the book, making sure the design is centred. Overlap the ends of the fabric inside the cover and secure with double-sided sticky tape or a suitable glue.

Lavender sachet

Materials

- Two pieces of 28-count white Quaker cloth (Zweigart 100), each 5 x 9in (12.5 x 23cm)
- DMC stranded cotton as listed in the key
- Size 26 tapestry needle
- Three lengths of assorted purple ribbon, 24in (60cm)
- Dried lavender
- Lace, 12in (30cm)
- Ribbon rosebud (optional)

Design size

1⅝ x 4⅞in (3.8 x 12.1cm) at 14-count

Stitch count

22 x 68

Method

1 Find the centre of your piece of fabric and begin stitching from here following the chart. Work the cross stitches over two threads of fabric.

2 Use two strands of thread for the three green shades and three strands for the purple shades as indicated in the key. There is no backstitch in this design.

3 Once you have completed the stitching, press the fabric.

4 Sew a small hem along the top of both pieces of fabric. Place the right sides together and stitch along the bottom and the sides. Turn the bag the right way, and stitch the lace along the top.

5 Fill the bag with dried lavender and tie a length of ribbon around the top to fasten. If you use one, stitch the ribbon rosebud into position.

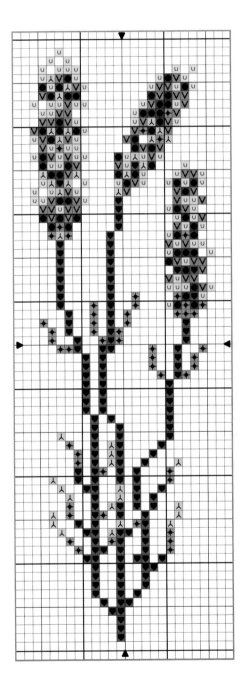

Thread key — DMC

Three strands

U	Lavender Light	211
●	Blue Violet Dark	333
V	Blue Violet Medium	340

Two strands

⅄	Green Light	3817
✦	Green Medium	3816
♥	Green Dark	561

Note: use two strands of the three shades of green cross stitch and three for the three shades of purple

Geranium and Sweet Pea Cards

Popular around the world, geranium includes members of the genus Pelargonium, and cranesbill. Pelargoniums originated in Africa but, in parts of Europe, preserved examples of the plant have been dated to the last ice age. The ivy-leaved variety has been used in brides' bouquets and is a very popular border and house plant.

The sweet pea has a fresh, sweet fragrance and is often grown in the garden as a climber. Sweet peas were used by the scientist Mendel in his experiments with genetics; he crossed many varieties thousands of times to prove his theories. His work has paved the way for genetic research and helped to provide an insight into heredity.

They can be stitched onto Aida. If you like, try out different -coloured fabrics against the threads to see which you prefer.

Materials

For each card:

- 28-count white evenweave 5in (12.8cm) square
- DMC stranded cotton as listed in the key
- Size 26 tapestry needle
- Three-fold card blank, 3½ x 4½in (8.9 x 11.4cm) with a circular aperture

VICTORIAN LANGUAGE OF FLOWERS

The geranium means comfort, although a pink geranium means doubt and a white one, indecision.

The sweet pea means tenderness.

Geranium card

Design size

1¾ x 1¾in (4.5 x 4.5cm) at 14-count

Stitch count

24 x 25

Sweet pea card

Design size

2⅜ x 2⅜in (6.4 x 6.4cm) at 14-count

Stitch count

33 x 33

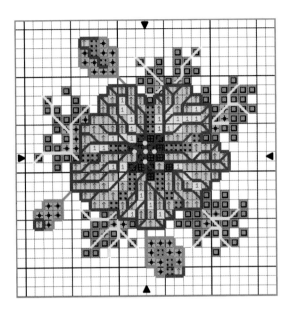

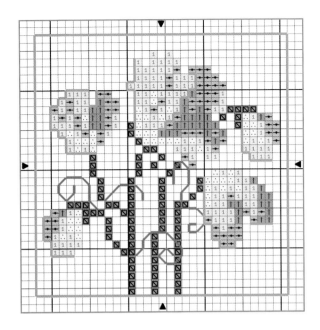

Thread key		DMC
1	Pink Light	818
⇑	Pink	605
	Pink Medium	603
	Mauve Dark	917
✛	Green Medium	368
▢	Green Dark	987

Backstitch		
	Mauve Dark	917
	Green Dark	987
	Green Light	3348

French knots		
●	Green Light	3348

Note: use two strands for cross stitch
and one for backstitch

Thread key		DMC
1	Pink Very Light	818
●	Rose Light	3716
◩	Green	562
∴	Yellow Light	3823
⇑	Rose	962

Backstitch		
	Green Dark	561
	Rose	962

Note: use two strands for cross stitch
and one for backstitch

Method

1 Stitch both designs in the same way. Find the centre of the fabric and begin stitching from here following the chart. Work the cross stitches over two threads of fabric.

2 Use two strands of thread for cross stitch and one for backstitch as indicated in the key.

3 Once you have completed the stitching, press the fabric.

4 Mount the design in the aperture of the card.

Lotus Coaster

The sacred lotus, *Nelumbo nucifera*, is a marginal plant that favours warm conditions. It has plate-shaped leaves and beautiful, pale, peachy-coloured flowers.

The lotus has been appropriated to mean many things. It is the national symbol for both Egypt and India where it symbolizes the universe, and the water in which it thrives is known as the water of life. It sometimes means a lost love.

The Chinese represent each of the seasons with a flower and the lotus symbolizes summer.

Stitched onto a white evenweave fabric, this coaster would look charming as a companion to the wake-robin coaster (see page 24). It is a simple design and ideal for beginners.

Stitch the design onto 14-count Aida to give the same dimensions. The design includes a little backstitch.

Materials

- 28-count white Quaker Cloth (Zweigart 100) 6in (15cm) square
- DMC stranded cotton as listed in the key
- Size 26 tapestry needle
- Framecraft coaster
- Lightweight iron-on interfacing, e.g. Vilene (optional)

Design size

2⅜ x 2⅜in (6.4 x 6.4cm) at 14-count

Stitch count

34 x 34

Method

1 Find the centre of the fabric and begin to stitch from here following the chart. Work the cross stitches over two threads of fabric.

2 Use two strands of thread for cross stitch, and one for backstitch as indicated in the key.

3 Once you have completed the stitching, press the fabric.

4 I recommend that you use lightweight iron-on interfacing or Vilene to back the work and prevent fraying.

5 Cut out the design to fit the coaster and mount it following the manufacturer's instructions.

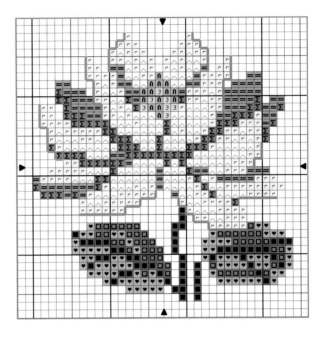

	Thread key	DMC
♥	Green Light	989
3	Yellow	744
∩	Burnt Orange	972
∧	White	BLANC
=	Coral	352
Σ	Coral Dark	351
☐	Green Medium	987
r	Peach	948
■	Green Dark	986

Backstitch

▬	Coral Dark	351

Note: use two strands for cross stitch and one for backstitch

Clematis Desk Set

This climbing plant is so versatile that with careful planting of different varieties you can fill your garden with a mass of different flowers from early spring through to late autumn. Clematis are usually classified by their flowering type into three groups: early flowering, early large flowering, and late large flowering. Clematis is a genus of evergreen and deciduous plants. It is often referred to as 'old man's beard'. Much underrated, I wouldn't be without clematis in my garden; it is excellent for climbing up fences and walls.

Both designs could alternatively be stitched and mounted in a card if you prefer. These designs contain fractional stitches, so I recommend an evenweave fabric as opposed to Aida, as it is easier to stitch with in this instance.

VICTORIAN LANGUAGE
OF FLOWERS

Clematis means mental beauty or intellectuality.

Clematis wooden bowl

Materials

- 28-count white Brittney (Zweigart 100), 6in (15cm) square
- DMC stranded cotton as listed in the key
- Size 26 tapestry needle
- Framecraft wooden bowl (WPBOX3)

Design size

1⅞ x 1⅞in (5 x 5cm) at 14-count

Stitch count

23 x 23

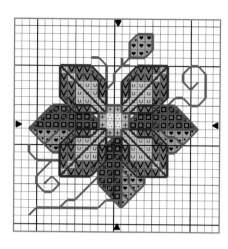

Method

1 Stitch both designs in the same way. Find the centre of the fabric and begin stitching from here following the chart. Work the cross stitches over two threads of fabric.

2 Work two strands of thread for cross stitch and one for backstitch as indicated in the key.

3 Once you have completed the stitching, press the fabric and mount following the manufacturer's instructions. I recommend that you use lightweight iron-on interfacing to back the work and prevent fraying.

4 Cut out the design to fit the lid of the bowl or desk tidy.

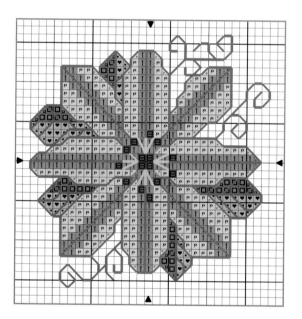

Thread key		DMC
U	Lavender Light	211
V	Blue Violet Medium	340
♥	Green	989
▢	Green Medium	987
∴	Yellow Light	3823
+	Yellow	726

Backstitch		
▬	Blue Violet Dark	333
▬	Green Dark	986

Note: use two strands for cross stitch and one for backstitch

Clematis desk tidy

Materials

- 28-count white Brittney (Zweigart 100), 6in (15cm) square
- DMC stranded cotton as listed in the key
- Size 26 tapestry needle
- Framecraft desk tidy (WDK)

Design size

2¼ x 2¼ (5.7 x 5.7cm) at 14-count

Stitch count

31 x 32

Thread key		DMC
℗	Dusty Rose	963
↑	Dusty Rose Medium	962
♥	Green	989
▢	Green Medium	987
▦	Mauve	3726

Backstitch		
▬	Cerise	3804
▬	Green Dark	986
▬	Green Pale	472

Note: use two strands for cross stitch and one for backstitch

Autumn

'Season of mists and mellow fruitfulness!
Close bosom-friend of the maturing sun;
Conspiring with him to load and bless
With fruits the vines that round the thatch-eaves run...'

(John Keats)

Heralding the end to summer, there is nothing to match the beauty of golden leaves strewn in soft drifts in an autumn woodland landscape.

For autumn, the white rose cushion is a stunning reminder that the season has its own beautiful blossoms. For beginners, the amaryllis card is ideal and a welcome gift to friends and family. Treat yourself to the red-hot poker bookmark, a colourful way to accompany your favourite book as you curl up by the fire on a cold evening to read.

Red-hot Poker Bookmark

The red-hot poker, or *Kniphofia uvaria,* is sometimes also known as the torch lily because of its shape and colour. This perennial can grow to a height of 3ft (1m). It has tall red and yellow spikes that flower in late summer and early autumn. It is a cottage-garden flower that makes a striking addition to the border, alongside other tall flowers such as delphiniums and foxgloves.

The red-hot poker is the perfect shape for a bookmark. I have stitched this simple design onto white Aida. It is an ideal project for the beginner. The design includes only a little backstitch and a few carefully chosen colours.

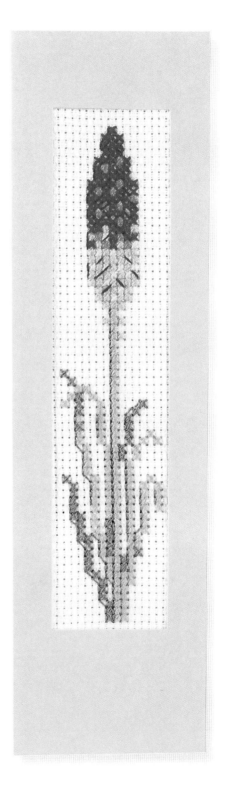

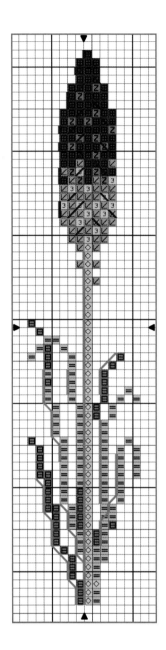

Thread key

			DMC
▦	Red Bright		666
◇	Green		704
=	Green Bright		907
⊟	Green Medium		905
3	Yellow		744
◸	Yellow Dark		742
Z	Orange		947

Backstitch

─	Green Medium		905
━	Garnet		815

Note: use two strands for cross stitch
and one for backstitch

Materials

- 14-count white Aida, 2 x 7in (5 x 17.5cm)
- DMC stranded cotton as listed in the key
- Size 26 tapestry needle
- Craft Creations square-ended bookmark,
  2 x 7in (5 x 17.5cm)

Design size

1 x 4¾in (2.5 x 12cm) at 14-count

Stitch count

14 x 66

Method

1 Find the centre of the fabric and begin stitching
   from here following the chart. Work the cross
   stitches over one block of fabric.

2 Use two strands of thread for cross stitch and one
   for backstitch as indicated in the key.

3 Once you have completed the stitching, press
   the fabric and mount in the bookmark following
   the same techniques for mounting a card (see
   page 11).

White Rose Cushion Cover

Roses have existed in the West for over 5000 years, but in China and Japan rose gardens can be dated back centuries earlier.

Roses today are classified into four types: ground cover, standard, climbing and bush, which includes hybrid tea, floribunda and shrub roses. While roses have been popular in England since the 1500s, it wasn't until the reign of Queen Victoria that varieties from Europe and the East were extensively hybridized to produce new and exciting varieties. As a result, the rose became one of the most popular garden flowers of the period, and continues to be a much-loved garden flower today.

I have made the white rose into a cushion design, but it can also be mounted in a square frame if you prefer. The design is suitable for a more advanced stitcher. The design can also be stitched onto 14-count Aida.

Materials

- 28-count Antique white Brittney (Zweigart), 14in (35cm) square
- DMC stranded cotton as listed in the key
- Size 26 tapestry needle
- Cushion pad, 18in (45cm) square
- Piece of cream fabric, 20in (50cm) square
- Two pieces of backing fabric, 20 x 11in (50 x 28cm)
- Zip, 12in (30cm) long
- Length of ribbon, 18in (45.5cm) (to trim)

Design size

7⅝ x 7⅝in (19 x 19cm) 14-count

Stitch count

106 x 107

Method

1. Find the centre of the fabric and begin stitching from here following the chart. Work the cross stitches over two threads of fabric.
2. Use two strands of thread for cross stitch and French knots, and one for backstitch as indicated in the key. I recommend that you use a thread sorter for this design as there are lots of similar shades.
3. Once you have completed the stitching, press the fabric.
4. Trim the evenweave to 10in (25cm), making sure that the design is centred. Use small zigzag stitches around the edges to prevent fraying. Stitch the design to the centre front of the cream fabric to form the front of the cushion.
5. Stitch the ribbon around each edge of the design, covering the zigzag stitches.
6. Stitch the two pieces of backing fabric together, and insert the zip.
7. With right sides facing, stitch the backing fabric and cushion front, allowing 1in (2.5cm) seams.
8. Press and insert the cushion pad.

Thread key

		DMC
◆	Green Light	470
◢	Brown	611
▣	Brown Dark	610
∧	Cream	712
▦	Tan	436
•	White Bright	B5200

		DMC
⪽	Green	988
◖	Green Dark	3345
◣	Grey	648
⫽	Brown Light	422
1	Ecru	ECRU
U	Beige	822

Backstitch

∼∼∼	Green Very Dark	895
———	Brown Grey	3022

French knots

●	Green Dark	3345

Note: use two strands for cross stitch and one for backstitch

Begonia Pincushion

Begonias are divided into a number of groups including deciduous and evergreen shrubs, trees, perennials and annuals. A versatile plant, the begonia favours slightly acidic soil, and varieties range from frost-tender to fully hardy.

A pincushion is a lovely gift idea for a stitcher. Using only whole cross stitches and no backstitch, this design is easy to stitch and quick to finish. Alternatively, mount the design in a square aperture card, omitting the border if you prefer.

Materials

- Two pieces of 28-count white evenweave, each 6in (15cm) square
- DMC stranded cotton as listed in the key
- Size 26 tapestry needle
- Wadding and cord (for finishing)

Design size

3⅝ x 3⅝ (8.9 x 8.9cm) at 14-count

Stitch count

50 x 50

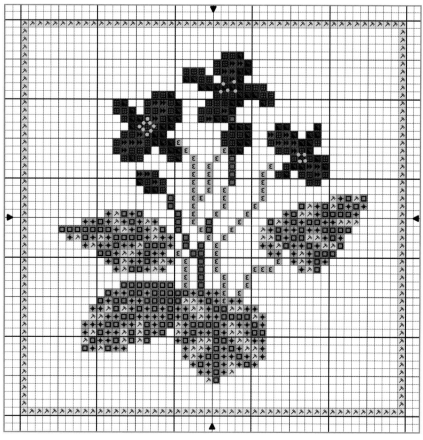

Method

1 Find the centre of the fabric and begin stitching from here following the chart. Work the cross stitches over two threads of fabric.

2 Use two strands of thread for cross stitch as indicated in the key.

3 Once you have completed the stitching, press the fabric.

4 Trim both pieces of fabric to 5in (12.5cm). With right sides facing, stitch the two pieces of fabric together, leaving a seam allowance of ½in (1.25cm) all the way around and a small opening for turning and stuffing.

5 Turn the cushion right side out and stuff with the wadding.

6 Slip stitch cord around each side of the cushion beginning at the opening, then insert the end of the cord into the opening. Once the cord has been stitched all round the cushion, insert the end into the opening and slip-stitch it closed.

Thread key		DMC
▶▶	Pink Dark	3705
⊞	Red Bright	666
◪	Red Dark	498
✚	Green	368
☐	Green Medium	987
⋏	Green Light	369
Ɛ	Old Gold	676
▨	Old Gold Dark	680

French knots

●	Yellow	743

Note: Use two strands for cross stitch

Anemone and Sunflower Pictures

The anemone is often called the windflower because it derives from the Greek *anemos*, which means 'wind'. As the name suggests, they do flourish in windy sites, although in fact it thrives in different sites all around the world. It first appeared in Britain after the Crusades, when travellers brought it back from the Middle East.

The Chinese call the anemone the 'flower of death' and, in ancient Egypt, where it can be dated back to about 1500 BC, it was considered a symbol of illness, perhaps because of the white flush at the base of the petals. Conversely, other cultures claim that it has important healing properties.

The simple beauty of this plant makes it popular to grow in the garden. Although mainly an autumn-flowering plant, some varieties flower in spring.

The sunflower, or *Helianthus,* is a late summer- or early autumn-flowering perennial. Reaching a gargantuan height of up to 3ft (90cm), the large, sunshine-coloured, daisy-like heads can be as much as 12in (30cm) in diameter.

The sunflower makes a cheering sight in any garden. However, it can be invasive and very fast-growing, so do be careful where you plant it.

These designs are simple to stitch. They include whole cross stitches and no backstitch. Stitched onto a white evenweave fabric, they can easily be stitched onto 14-count white Aida. I have chosen picture frames with mounts but, if you like, omit the mount and use 6 x 8in (15 x 20cm) frames instead.

Materials

For each picture:

- 28-count white Quaker Cloth (Zweigart 100), 9 x 11in (23 x 28cm)
- DMC stranded cotton as listed in the key
- Size 26 tapestry needle
- Frame, 4 x 6in (10 x 15cm)

Anemone

Design size

2⅝ x 4⅝in (6.4 x 11.4cm) at 14-count

Stitch count

37 x 64

	Thread key	DMC
▪	White	BLANC
Ɛ	Pink Light	761
∅	Pink Dark	3831
▲	Pink Medium	3833
■	Black	310
▼	Green Medium	562
▷	Green Dark	561
f	Green Light	164
◪	Grey Dark	317

Note: use two strands for cross stitch

Sunflower

Design size

2½ x 4⅝in (6.4 x 11.4cm) at 14-count

Stitch count

35 x 65

Method

1 Stitch both designs in the same way. Find the centre of the fabric and begin stitching from here following the chart. Work the cross stitches over two threads of fabric.

2 Use two strands of thread for cross stitch as indicated in the key.

3 Once you have completed the stitching, press the fabric and mount within your chosen frame.

Thread key		DMC
♥	Green	989
◻	Green Medium	987
⊟	Brown	3826
✳	Brown Medium	975
◘	Brown	801
2	Yellow Light	727
+	Yellow	726
∩	Yellow Dark	972
↖	Green Light	3348

Note: use two strands for cross stitch

Amaryllis Card

These pretty autumn-flowering bulbs should be grown in a south-facing patch for best results; they are not very frost-hardy. The exquisite trumpet- or funnel-shaped flowers are so beautiful that they are worth the extra effort required to grow them.

When the Victorians sent the amaryllis to someone it was intended as a special extension of friendship.

This simple card design contains no text and can be framed in its mount using a standard size 6 x 8in (15 x 20cm) frame.

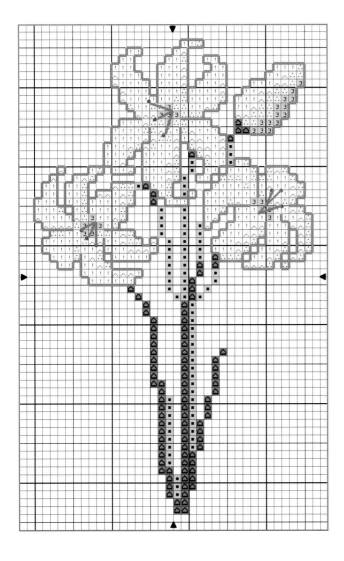

Materials

- 28-count baby blue Cashel linen (Zweigart 562), 6 x 8in (15 x 20cm)
- DMC stranded cotton as listed in the key
- Size 26 tapestry needle
- Three-fold card blank, 6 x 8in (15 x 20cm), with an oval aperture

Design size

2⅝ x 4¼in (6.4 x 10.8cm) at 14-count

Stitch count

36 x 60

Method

1 Find the centre of the fabric and begin stitching from here following the chart. Work the cross stitches over two threads of fabric.

2 Use two strands of thread for cross stitch and French knots, and one for backstitch as indicated in the key.

3 Once you have completed the stitching, press the fabric and mount in a card blank.

	Thread key	DMC
!	White Bright	B5200
∴	Yellow Light	3078
∧	Cream	746
⌂	Green	581
■	Green Light	3819
3	Yellow	744

	Backstitch	
—	Green	581
—	Green Dark	904

	French knots	
●	Mahogany	301

Note: use two strands for cross stitch and French knots and one for backstitch

Chrysanthemum Coaster

The chrysanthemum means cheerfulness and optimism, wealth and happiness.

In Australia, a white chrysanthemum is worn on Mother's Day as a sign of respect and celebration. In Japan, it was declared many centuries ago that only royalty was allowed to wear the chrysanthemum, and it is now their national flower.

For the Chinese, the chrysanthemum is the flower symbol for the season of autumn.

I have mounted the chrysanthemum head in a coaster. This is the third coaster that you can make, one for each season. The design is ideal for the beginner, is simple to stitch and includes whole cross stitches and only a little backstitch.

Materials

- 28-count white evenweave fabric, 6in (15cm) square
- DMC stranded cotton as listed in the key
- Size 26 tapestry needle
- Framecraft coaster

Design size

2⅝ x 2⅝in (6.4 x 6.4cm) at 14-count

Stitch count

36 x 36

Method

1   Find the centre of the fabric and begin stitching from here following the chart. Work the cross stitches over two threads of fabric.

2   Use two strands of thread for cross stitch and one for backstitch as indicated in the key.

3   Once you have completed the stitching, press the fabric and mount in your chosen frame, referring to the manufacturer's instructions.

4   I recommend that you use lightweight iron-on interfacing or Vilene to back the work and prevent fraying.

5   Cut out the design to fit the coaster.

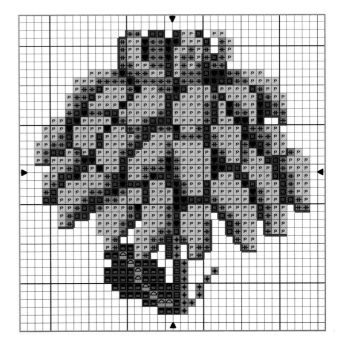

Thread key		DMC
p	Rose	963
╫	Pink Medium	3706
▣	Pink Dark	3705
▼	Red	817
▤	Cocoa	3860
✛	Cocoa Light	452
◠	Green Light	368
▣	Green	367

Backstitch

—	Red	817

Note: use two strands for cross stitch and one for backstitch

Lily and Aster Embroidery Set

The lily dates back at least to Roman times. For the early Christians, the white lily was a symbol of purity, and is associated with the Madonna. Jesus said, 'consider how the lilies grow… I tell you not even King Solomon in his entire splendour was dressed as beautifully as these.' (Luke 12:27).

The aster, or Michaelmas daisy as it is also known, is a daisy-like perennial which flowers between summer and late autumn and is available in a variety of colours. This pretty flower is linked to the month of October.

VICTORIAN LANGUAGE
OF FLOWERS
The lily means
purity
The aster means
regret or truth.

These simple, delicate designs would make delightful gifts. The two floral designs do contain fractional cross stitches and some backstitch. They would ideally suit a stitcher with some experience, but beginners shouldn't be put off; they can always practise some fractional cross stitches on a scrap of fabric first.

Lily workbox

Materials

- 28-count white Brittney (Zweigart 100), 7 x 9in (17.5 x 23cm)
- DMC stranded cotton as listed in the key
- Size 26 tapestry needle
- Impress workbox (0056)

Design size

2⅞ x 5⅛in (7.3 x 13cm) at 14-count

Stitch count

41 x 71

Aster wooden pincushion

Materials

- 28-count white Brittney (Zweigart 100), 6in (15cm) square
- DMC stranded cotton as listed in the key
- Size 26 tapestry needle
- Wooden pincushion supplied by Impress (0067)

Design size

2¼ x 2¼in (5.7 x 5.7cm) at 28-count

Stitch count

32 x 32

	Thread key	DMC
1	Pink Very Light	818
p	Dusty Rose Light	963
-•-	Dusty Rose	3716
✚	Pistachio Green	368
f	Green Light	772
⊞	Pistachio Green Dark	367
◹	Pink Dark	602

	Thread key	DMC
	Backstitch	
	Green Light	772
	Pink Dark	602
	Dusty Rose Medium	962
	French knots	
●	Garnet	221

Note: Use two strands for cross stitch and one for backstitch

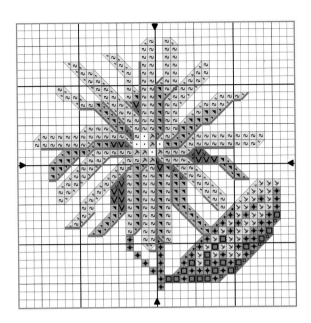

Thread key

		DMC
◥	Blue Violet	341
V	Blue Violet Medium	156
✚	Green	368
℧	Blue Violet Light	3747
⚔	Yellow	743
•	Yellow Light	3823
⑂	Green Light	369
▣	Green Medium	320

Backstitch

▬	Blue Violet Medium	156
▬	Cornflower Blue	3807

Note: use two strands for cross stitch
and one for backstitch

Method

1 Stitch both designs in the same way. Find the centre of the fabric and begin stitching from here following the chart. Work the cross stitches over two threads of fabric.

2 Use two strands of thread for cross stitch and two for French knots. Stitch the lily stamens using two threads in long stitch. The rest of the backstitch should be stitched using one strand of thread as indicated in the key. When stitching the fractional stitches in the aster, the paler petals should be stitched as three-quarter cross stitches as they are in front of the darker petals, and the darker petals as quarter cross stitches. This will add depth to the design.

3 Once you have completed the stitching, press the fabric.

4 To mount in your chosen box or wooden pincushion, refer to the manufacturer's instructions.

5 I have sandwiched wadding between the fabric and backing board to give a raised effect. It also serves to add padding to the lid if you are going to use either box for keeping pins.

6 Using the backing board provided, cut out a piece of wadding the same size and glue to the board. Centre the designs over both the board and wadding and use either double-sided tape or a suitable glue to secure the fabric to the board.

7 Assemble following the manufacturer's instructions, omitting the acetate if you are making a pincushion.

Fuchsia Picture

uchsias grow around the world, from the Andes to New Zealand, but were not introduced to Britain until the 1700s. Flowering between early summer and autumn, this genus has bell-shaped flowers that are often bicoloured. Trailing varieties are ideal plants for hanging baskets – a common sight in gardens today. There are also shrub and tree varieties.

This stunning design has been stitched on a simple white 14-count Aida fabric and mounted in a frame.

If you prefer, the design can be stitched onto 28-count white evenweave fabric, stitching over two threads of fabric to give the same size. If you are stitching this design to display with other pictures, then use the same fabric for each design – either evenweave or Aida – so that the designs coordinate.

Materials

- 14-count white Aida, 12 x 14in (30 x 35cm)
- DMC stranded cotton as listed in the key
- Size 26 tapestry needle
- Frame, 8 x 10in (20 x 30cm), mount with an aperture, 6 x 8in (15 x 20cm)

Design size

5⅜ x 7¼in (14 x 18.4cm) at 14-count

Stitch count

75 x 101

Method

1. Find the centre of the fabric and begin stitching from here following the chart. Work the cross stitches over one block of fabric.

2. Use two strands of thread for cross stitch and French knots, and one for backstitch as indicated in the key. I recommend that you use a thread sorter for this design to avoid confusing the three different shades of pink and purple.

3. Once you have completed the stitching, press the fabric and mount in your chosen frame. If you don't want to use a mount, substitute with a 6 x 8in (15 x 20cm) frame.

Thread key

		DMC				DMC
U	Lavender Light	153	↖	Green Light	3348
O	Mauve	3607	⊥	Green	470
L	Mauve Light	3608	☐	Green Dark	987
+	Violet	554	✳	Cocoa Light	452
◆	Violet Medium	553	⧄	Cocoa Dark	451
●	Violet Very Dark	550			

Backstitch

		DMC
▬▬	Violet Very Dark	550
▬▬	Brown	779

French knots

		DMC
●	Violet Very Dark	550

Note: use two strands for cross stitch
and two for backstitch

Dahlia Paperweight

Dahlias are autumn-flowering perennials, often grown as pretty bedding plants and also for competitions. They are available in a multitude of colours but, perhaps oddly, they are all colours from the warm end of the palette; there are no blue species.

Dahlias are associated with the month of August.

This simple design uses only cross stitch and no backstitch. It looks effective stitched on white 14-count Aida fabric and mounted in a paperweight. Keep it for yourself or make it a gift for someone special; you can adapt the design to mount it in a small circular-aperture card for a friend whose birthday is in the month of August.

Materials

- 14-count white Aida 5in (12.5cm)
- DMC stranded cotton as listed in the key
- Size 26 tapestry needle
- Framecraft paperweight (PW3)

Design size

1¾ x 1¾in (4.5 x 4.5cm) at 14-count

Stitch count

25 x 25

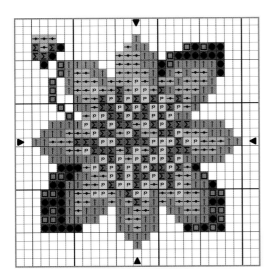

Method

1 Find the centre of the fabric and begin stitching from here following the chart. Work the cross stitches over one block of fabric.

2 Use two strands of thread for cross stitch as indicated in the key.

3 Once you have completed the stitching, press the fabric.

4 I recommend that you use lightweight iron-on interfacing or Vilene to back the work and prevent fraying.

5 Use the paper disc provided as a template. Centre the disc over the stitching and draw around it with a pencil. Cut out along the pencil line. The fabric should fit inside the bottom recess of the paperweight.

6 Assemble following the manufacturer's instructions.

Thread key	DMC
↑ Rose Medium	962
•– Rose	3716
P Rose Light	963
Σ Raspberry	3832
☐ Green	320
● Green Dark	319

Note: use two strands for cross stitch

Cyclamen Photograph Album

The name cyclamen derives from the Greek word *kyklos* meaning 'circular', probably because of the shape of the leaves or petals. Cyclamens grow from tubers and prefer rich soil and partial shade; for this reason they flourish in woodland areas.

VICTORIAN LANGUAGE
OF FLOWERS

*The cyclamen
means
indifference.*

This design looks very pretty on the front of a photograph album, but you can also adapt the design and stitch it as a card or mount it in a small frame. Only whole cross stitches are used in this design and no backstitch, making it a very simple project.

Materials

- 28-count white Brittney (Zweigart 100), 6in (15cm) square
- DMC stranded cotton as listed in the key
- Size 26 tapestry needle
- Suitable photograph album or notebook
- Ribbon or cord (to trim)
- Glue or double-sided sticky tape

Design size

2⅝ x 3½in (6.4 x 8.9cm) at 14-count

Stitch count

36 x 49

Method

1 Find the centre of the fabric and begin stitching from here following the chart. Work the cross stitches over two threads of fabric.
2 Use two strands of thread for cross stitch as indicated in the key.
3 Once you have completed the stitching, press the fabric.
4 Back the cyclamen with medium-weight iron-on Vilene. Trim the fabric to neaten. Making sure the design is centred, attach to the front cover of the photo album using double-sided sticky tape or glue.
5 Attach ribbon or cord around the four edges using glue.

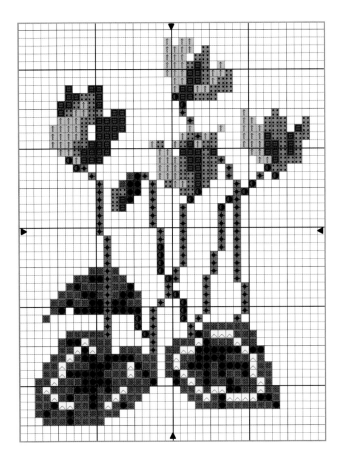

	Thread key	DMC
⇑	Pink	605
	Pink Medium	603
	Pink Dark	601
●	Green Dark	500
	Green	502
∧	Cream	712
	Brown	632
✦	Brown Light	407

Note: use two strands for cross stitch

Winter

'Ev'n winter bleak has charms to me,
When winds rave thro' the naked tree;
Or frosts on hills of Ochiltree
Are hoary gray;
Or blinding drifts wild furious flee,
Dark'ning the day!'

(Robert Burns)

Winter conjures images of snow and stark leafless branches, the bright red berries of the holly and its evergreen leathery leaves come into their own. The delicate blush of the Christmas rose is beautiful in any setting. My favorites have to be the flowering bulbs that can be found from late autumn right through to early spring the graceful snowdrop and the goblet-shaped crocus look stunning peeping through snow, planted in drifts of colour.

The holly card and the poinsettia and holly cake band make the perfect festive decoration. Try stitching the Christmas rose keepsake box for someone special; it is ideal for keeping treasured objects.

Pansy and Snowdrop Pictures

The delicate nodding heads of the snowdrop signal that winter is almost at an end. Peeping through the snow, these tiny flowers are one of the first bulbs to appear after a long winter's sleep; they bring life to the garden. The common snowdrop, *Galanthus nivalis*, which flowers in January and February, was once seen in abundance in British woodland, but these 'fair maids of February' as they are affectionately called, have now become a rare sight.

The bright velvety petals of the pansy feature in gardens between late autumn and spring in combinations of purples, blues, yellows and whites. It is a member of the viola, or violet, family. The pansy is the birthday flower of June. In the Victorian language of flowers it means 'thoughts', probably because the name 'pansy' is thought to derive from the French verb *penser*, to think.

These little pictures could be mounted as cards to celebrate a winter birthday or to send as a notelet to someone special. Try stitching the snowdrop onto a cream-coloured fabric for a more subtle effect. Both designs include whole cross stitches only and no backstitch, making them perfect for the beginner.

VICTORIAN LANGUAGE
OF FLOWERS

The snowdrop means hope and consolation, and the pansy means to think of someone

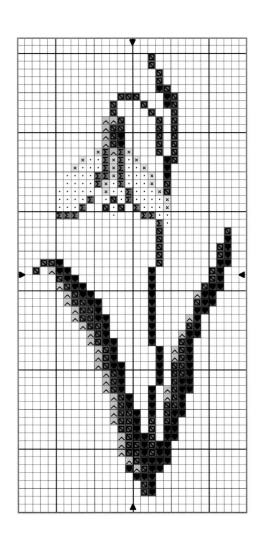

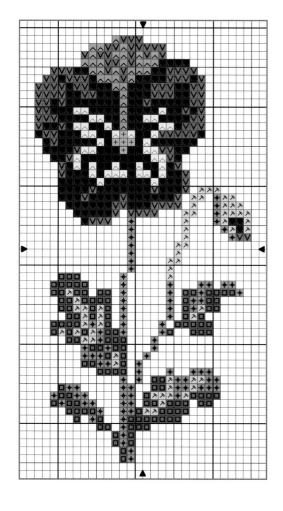

Thread key	DMC
▼ Green Dark	561
∧ Green Light	164
◨ Green Medium	562
· White Bright	B5200
× Grey Light	168
Σ Grey Blue	926

Note: use two strands for cross stitch
and one for backstitch

Thread key	DMC
∧ Lavender	210
● Violet Dark	550
∨ Blue Violet	340
▼ Blue Violet Dark	333
⚒ Green Light	369
✚ Green Medium	368
▢ Green Dark	987
∧ White	BLANC
✚ Yellow	726

Note: use two strands for cross stitch
and one for backstitch

Snowdrop

Materials

- Lilac 28-count Cashel linen (Zweigart 558) 7 x 9in (17.5 x 23cm)
- DMC stranded threads as listed in the key
- Size 26 tapestry needle
- Frame with an aperture, 6 x 4in (15 x 10cm)

Design size

1⅞ x 4in (4.6 x 10cm) at 14-count

Stitch count

26 x 56

Pansy

Materials

- White 28-count evenweave fabric, 7 x 9in (17.5 x 23cm)
- DMC stranded thread as listed in the key
- Size 26 tapestry needle
- Frame with an aperture 6 x 4in (15 x 10cm)

Design size

2 x 3⅞in (5 x 9.7cm) at 14-count

Stitch count

28 x 54

Method

1 Stitch both designs in the same way. Find the centre of the fabric and begin stitching from here following the chart. Work the cross stitches over two threads of fabric.

2 Use two strands of thread as indicated in the key. No backstitch is required for these designs.

3 Once you have completed the stitching, press the fabric.

4 Mount the design in your chosen frame. The dimensions of the finished designs make them ideal for 6 x 4in (15 x 10cm) standard frames or cards with the same-size aperture. See page 11 for finishing techniques.

Crocus Picture

On the tail of the snowdrops, the bright goblet-shaped yellow and purple flowers of the crocus bring cheer to a cold winter's day and signify that spring is close at hand. Although mainly winter-flowering, careful selection of different species when planting ensures that flowers appear from late autumn through to early spring. Plant them in drifts to achieve the best effect.

This pretty picture has been mounted with a triple aperture and stitched onto an antique white evenweave fabric to stunning effect. This simple design includes no backstitch and only whole cross stitch. Stitch a single crocus if you wish and mount in a small frame or card. Alternatively, stitch the pansy, snowdrop and a crocus (the purple would look nice) instead of three crocuses, and frame together in a triple frame.

Materials

- 28-count antique white Brittney (Zweigart 101), 21 x 14in (53 x 35cm)
- DMC stranded cotton as listed in the key
- Size 26 tapestry needle
- Frame with a triple mount, each aperture 4 x 6in (10 x 15cm)

Design size
10⅝ x 4in (26.6 x 10cm) at 14-count

Stitch count
149 x 56

VICTORIAN LANGUAGE
OF FLOWERS

The crocus means happiness and joy.

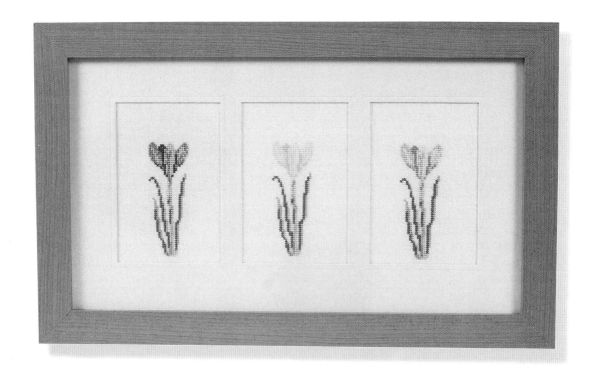

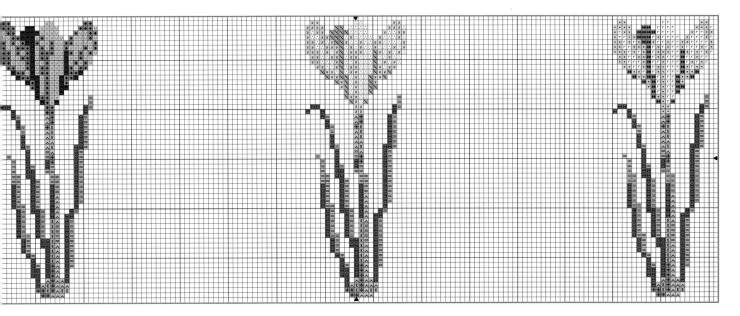

Method

1. Find the centre of the fabric and begin stitching from here following the chart. Work the cross stitches over two threads of fabric.

2. Use two strands of thread for cross stitch as indicated in the key.

3. I recommend that you complete the yellow crocus first, and measure out from the centre to either side to centre the purple and blue crocuses in your chosen mount. Double-check that the measurements correspond to your own frame and make any minor necessary adjustments. A good tip is to place the fabric with the yellow crocus complete underneath your mount and mark with pins the centre of the left and right aperture to place the other two crocuses. Start stitching from here, making sure that you correctly position the designs both horizontally and vertically. Double-check, too, that the fabric quantity I have used for my frame is also enough for your own. I have used a standard-sized frame and mount rather than a bespoke one.

4. Once you have completed the stitching, press the fabric.

5. Mount the pieces in the chosen frame. You may need to have a mount professionally cut, although mine was included with the frame (see page 11 for finishing techniques). The pictures can also be stitched and framed separately in three 4 x 6in (10 x 15cm) frames.

	Thread key	DMC
✳	Violet Grey	3042
U	Lavender Light	211
◆	Lavender	209
▣	Lavender Dark	3837
⊟	Green Dark	905
=	Green	907
⋀	Green Pale	472
Ɛ	Violet Grey Light	3743
∴	Yellow Light	3078
2	Yellow Medium	727
⟍	Yellow Dark	725
r	Blue Light	3756
●	Blue	3841
⊞	Blue Medium	3755

Note: use two strands for cross stitch

Peace Lily Card

Spathiphyllum is a genus of evergreen perennials, which grow from rhizomes. They favour warm, humid climates. *Spathiphyllum wallisii*, or peace lily, as it is more commonly known (although it is not actually a lily), is often grown as a houseplant or in the conservatory rather than in the garden. Although I grow mine in a pot on the patio in summer, I do bring it indoors in winter to protect it from frost.

This plant has unusually shaped, beautifully fragranced white flowers and glossy leaves. It is also known as white sails, and it is easy to see why.

This pretty design is stitched onto a green evenweave fabric and mounted in a card. There are only whole cross stitches and a little backstitch in this design, making it quick and simple to stitch. You can also use 14-count Aida.

Materials

- 28-count mint Cashel linen (Zweigart 633), 6½ x 8½in (16.5 x 21.6cm)
- DMC stranded cotton as listed in the key
- Size 26 tapestry needle
- Craft Creations card blank, 6 x 8in (15 x 20cm) with an oval aperture

Design size

2¼ x 4in (5.7 x 10cm) at 14-count

Stitch count

31 x 56

Method

1 Find the centre of the fabric and begin stitching from here following the chart. Work the cross stitches over two threads of fabric.
2 Use two strands of thread for cross stitch and one for backstitch as indicated in the key.
3 Once you have completed the stitching, press the fabric, trim and mount in the card blank.

	Thread key	DMC
H	Green Light	369
●	Green Dark	890
✕	Green Medium	367
+	Tan Light	738
1	Ecru	ECRU
·	White Bright	B5200
Ɛ	Grey Medium	415
O	Grey Dark	414
V	Tan	436

Backstitch

—	Grey Dark	414
—	Tan	436
—	Brown	435

Note: use two strands for cross stitch and one for backstitch

Christmas Rose Set

The Christmas rose, or *Helleborus niger,* is one of a family of plants which includes about 20 species, most of which are winter- and spring-flowering. For the romans, the word *helleborus* meant madness and, throughout history, this plant was prescribed as a cure for insanity. It was also used as a way to counteract poisoning by ingestion, as it induces vomiting. Surprisingly, however, many varieties are themselves actually poisonous.

This pair of designs lends an attractive festive touch to the home. They contain only whole cross stitch and a little backstitch.

The keepsake box is ideal for keeping photographs or other treasures safely tucked away. Stitch it for yourself or as a gift for someone special. The doily is stitched using waste canvas; if you have never used waste canvas before, then I suggest that you practise on a scrap of spare fabric first. (Doily kindly supplied by Debbie Cripps.)

Thread key

		DMC			
◆	Green Dark	470	◇ Yellow	726	**Backstitch**
Z	Green Medium	471	Ɛ Green Pale	472	Shell Pink 224
1	Ecru	ECRU	• White Bright	B5200	Green Very Dark 904
∿	Shell Pink Light	225	I Brown	3859	
▲	Shell Pink	224			

Note: use two strands for cross stitch
and one for backstitch

Keepsake box

Materials

- 14-count ivory Aida (Zweigart 400), 8 x 10in (20 x 25cm)
- DMC stranded cotton as listed in the key
- Size 26 tapestry needle
- The Viking Loom wooden box with an aperture, 5 x 7in (12.5 x 17.5cm)

Design size

3¾ x 5⅝in (9.5 x 14cm) at 14-count

Stitch count

52 x 78

Method

1 Find the centre of the fabric and begin stitching from here following the chart. Work the cross stitches over one block of fabric.

2 Use two strands of thread for cross stitch and one for backstitch as indicated in the key.

3 Once you have completed the cross stitches, press the fabric and mount in the chosen box lid following the manufacturer's instructions, using the same techniques to frame a picture (see page 11). The picture can also be mounted in a frame if you wish.

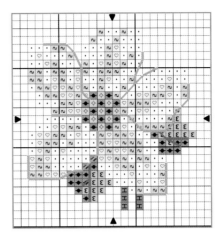

Thread key		DMC
✧	Yellow	726
·	White Bright	B5200
♡	Ecru	ECRUT
◆	Green Dark	470
2	Shell Pink Light	225
ε	Green Pale	472
⊥	Brown	3859

Backstitch		
▬	Shell Pink	224
▬	Green Very Dark	904

Note: use two strands for cross stitch and one for backstitch

Christmas rose doily

Materials

- DMC stranded cotton as listed in the key
- Size 28 tapestry needle
- Spare piece of 14-count canvas, approximately 3in (7.5cm) square

Design size

1½ x 1⅝in (3.8 x 3.8cm) at 14-count

Stitch count

22 x 23

Method

1 Tack the waste canvas to the centre of the doily. Find the centre of the waste canvas and begin stitching from here following the chart. Work the cross stitches over one block of fabric. Use two strands of thread for cross stitch and one for backstitch as indicated in the key.

2 Once you have completed the cross stitches, dampen the waste canvas and remove each thread with tweezers following the manufacturer's instructions, then press the doily. Alternatively, the design can be mounted in a trinket pot, coaster or card if you prefer.

Freesia Picture

Freesias are winter- and spring-flowering plants, grown from corms. They have beautiful, funnel-shaped flowers and a strong perfume, making them popular flowers for arrangements and in bouquets. The stems grow up to 12in (30cm) in height and become laden with pretty blooms, so much so that the stems seem to bend with their weight.

This design has been stitched onto a white evenweave fabric to create a simple effect. The design contains whole cross stitches only, making it accessible for beginners.

VICTORIAN LANGUAGE
OF FLOWERS

The freesia means innocence and 'love at first sight'.

Materials

- 28-count white Quaker cloth (Zweigart 100), 8 x 10in (20 x 25cm)
- DMC stranded cotton as listed in the key
- Size 26 tapestry needle
- Frame, 6 x 8in (15 x 20cm), with a mount and an aperture, 4 x 6in (10 x 15cm)

Design size

3⅛ x 5¾in (7.6 x 14.6cm) at 14-count

Stitch count

43 x 80

Method

1 Find the centre of the fabric and begin stitching from here following the chart. Work the cross stitches over two threads of fabric.

2 Use two strands of thread as indicated in the key. There is no backstitch required in this design.

3 Once you have completed the stitching, press the fabric and mount in your chosen frame. For finishing techniques, see page 11.

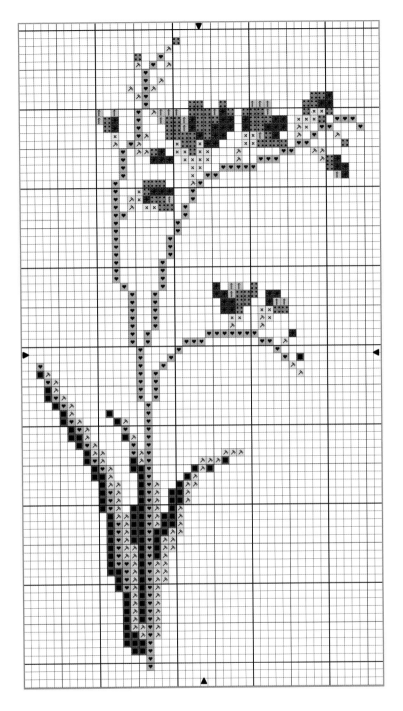

Thread key

		DMC
♥	Green	989
■	Green Dark	986
⋏	Green Light	369
⇑	Pink	605

		DMC
▦	Pink Medium	603
✹	Pink Dark	600
✕	Yellow Light	745

Note: use two strands for cross stitch

Poinsettia Coaster

The red leaflike bracts of this unusual plant are also found in shades of yellow, pink or white. They surround the tiny yellowy-green flowers that, quite unlike other flowers, lack petals. The poinsettia favours a warm climate and can be found growing in abundance around the Mediterranean. The flower is sometimes connected with the month of July.

Stitched on a cream evenweave fabric, this pretty coaster can be completed in just a few hours. It is the last in the set of four coasters representing the seasons.

VICTORIAN LANGUAGE
OF FLOWERS

The poinsettia means hope.

Materials

- 28-count cream Quaker cloth (Zweigart 222), 6in (15cm) square
- DMC stranded cotton as listed in the key
- Size 26 tapestry needle
- Framecraft coaster

Design size

2⅞ x 2⅞in (7.6 x 7.6cm) at 14-count

Stitch count

41 x 40

Method

1. Find the centre of the fabric and begin stitching from here following the chart. Work the cross stitches over two threads of fabric.
2. Use two strands of thread for cross stitch and one for backstitch as indicated in the key.
3. Once you have completed the stitching, press the fabric .
4. Mount the design in the coaster.
5. I recommend that you use lightweight iron-on interfacing or Vilene to back the work to prevent fraying before cutting it out to fit the coaster.

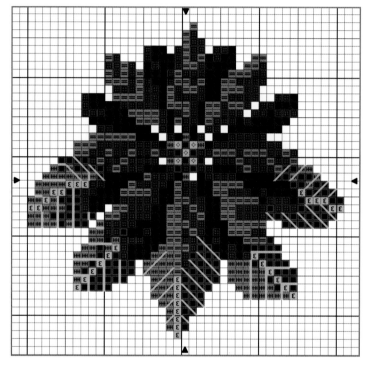

Thread key		DMC
●	Garnet	816
	Red Bright	666
=	Coral	352
■	Green Dark	986
Ɛ	Green Pale	472
⧓	Green	988
◇	Yellow	726

Backstitch		
	Green Pale	472

Note: use two strands for cross stitch and one for backstitch

Holly Card and Mistletoe Gift Tag

istletoe has a special celebratory place of its own. A Christmas tradition is to hang mistletoe from above and steal kisses from anyone who stands beneath it. Its roots are in the Victorian tradition of the kissing bough, which was hung somewhere special and a berry removed for every kiss given and received until the branch was empty.

Further back still, it was used as part of pagan festivities, because evergreens symbolized rebirth and fertility. It was banned from the Christian church because of these associations. Instead, the early

Christian church appropriated holly as a symbol of eternal life; the prickly leaves represent the crown of thorns and the red berries drops of blood. It was hung in churches at Christmas time.

Quite differently, the Native Americans used holly to make a tea to treat measles.

This pretty card and gift tag are simple to stitch, using only a few colours each. They are ideal for beginners. The mistletoe gift tag contains a few fractional stitches. Try stitching the designs onto napkins and table place mats for the festive season.

VICTORIAN LANGUAGE
OF FLOWERS

Holly means foresight.

Mistletoe means to overcome difficulties.

Holly card

Materials

- 28-count white evenweave fabric, 5 x 7in (12.5 x 17.5cm)
- DMC stranded cotton as listed in the key
- Size 26 tapestry needle
- Craft Creations three-fold card blank, 6 x 8in (15 x 20cm), with a circular aperture

Design size

2⅜ x 3½in (6.4 x 8.9cm) at 14-count

Stitch count

33 x 48

Method

1 Find the centre of the fabric and begin stitching from here following the chart. Work the cross stitches over two threads of fabric.
2 Use two strands of thread for cross stitch and one for backstitch as indicated in the key.
3 Once you have completed the stitching, press the fabric and mount in your chosen card blank.

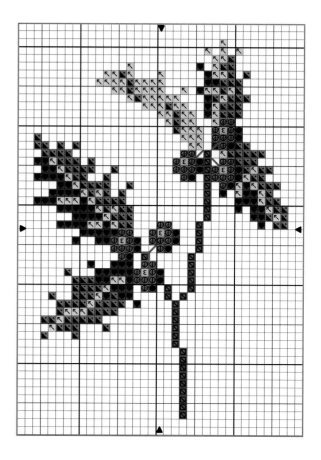

Thread key

		DMC
◐	Red Bright	666
●	Garnet	816
◣	Green Medium	3346
▼	Green Dark	895
↖	Green Light	3348
◻	Sage Green	580
Ɛ	Peach	353

Backstitch

▬	Sage Green	580

Note: Use two strands for cross stitch and two for backstitch

Mistletoe gift tag

Materials
- 28-count white evenweave fabric, 3 x 3½in (7.5 x 9cm)
- DMC stranded cotton as listed in the key
- Size 26 tapestry needle
- Green corrugated card, 3 x 3½in (7.5 x 9cm)
- Double-sided sticky tape or glue
- Hole puncher
- Ribbon

Design size
1⅛ x 1⅝in (2.8 x 3.8cm) at 14-count

Stitch count
15 x 20

Method
1 Find the centre of the fabric and begin stitching from here following the chart. Work the cross stitches over two threads of fabric.
2 Use two strands of thread for cross stitch and one for backstitch as indicated in the key.
3 After all the stitches have been completed, press the fabric.
4 Trim the fabric to 2 x 2½in (5 x 6.5cm). Remove a few threads around all four sides for a frayed appearance.
5 Attach the patch to the card using double-sided sticky tape or glue. Punch a hole in the top corner of the card and thread the ribbon through.

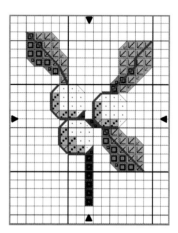

Thread key		DMC
	Green	989
	Green Medium	987
	Cream	712
	Beige Grey	644
	Brown Grey	3021

Backstitch

	Brown Grey	3021

Note: use two strands for cross stitch and one for backstitch

Ivy Plant Decoration

Ivy belongs to the genus Hedera, an evergreen climber which entwines itself around other plants and supports. Because of this, some believe the ivy to be parasitic (although it isn't), and the fact that it grows so fast often deters people from growing it, too. Often linked to everlasting life, the ivy also is said to contain healing properties. It can cure skin ailments and, if infused in boiling water and inhaled, relieve cold symptoms – although it might be wise to find out more before you do so!

VICTORIAN LANGUAGE
OF FLOWERS

Ivy means friendship and fidelity, and it was often sent as a proposal of marriage.

For centuries, ivy has been associated with the Christmas season. There is a well-known English carol called 'The Holly and the Ivy' written about it that celebrates the plant and its wintry context.

This design is very simple to stitch but will brighten up any plant pot. The Aida band could be stitched to a blind, a towel, or even used as a tie-back for curtains. Repeat the design along the length of a piece of Aida band to the desired length.

Materials

- White Aida band (Zweigart E7107), 26 stitches wide and 15in (37.5cm) long, or the same-size circumference as your plant pot, plus an extra 1in (2.5cm)
- DMC stranded cotton as listed in the key
- Size 26 tapestry needle
- Plant pot

Design size

1¾ x 7⅝in (4.5 x 19cm) at 14-count

Stitch count

24 x 106

Method

1 Find the centre of the fabric and begin stitching from here following the chart. Work the cross stitches over one block of fabric.

2 Use three strands of thread as indicated in the key.

3 Once you have completed the stitching, press the fabric and wrap it around the plant pot. Overlap the ends of the fabric and secure with double-sided sticky tape or glue.

4 You may find it easier to begin by folding the fabric in half lengthways, measuring down three stitches from the top and starting to stitch the first leaf from here. Find the same place on the chart and continue to read the chart as usual. This should ensure your design is centred. If stitching for a large plant pot, you may have to repeat the design along the Aida band.

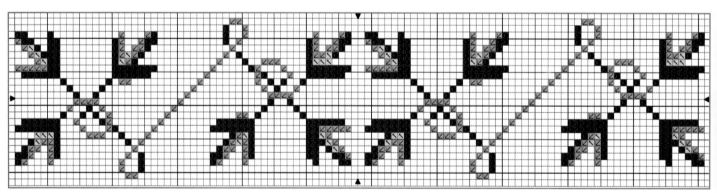

Thread key	DMC
◿ Green Medium	989
◑ Green Dark	986
◤ Green Light	3348

Note: use two strands for cross stitch and one for backstitch

Poinsettia and Holly Cake Band

In the northern hemisphere, we tend to think of Christmas as wintry, but for those in the southern hemisphere, it falls during the summer. The cake band is a traditional English Christmas design, but you could use it on any kind of cake you like to celebrate almost every occasion.

Stitched here onto Aida band, these pretty motifs could be stitched individually onto anything you wish; use them to cheer up napkins or place mats, for example. There are only five coloured threads in this design, and whole cross stitch only is utilised, making it relatively simple to complete.

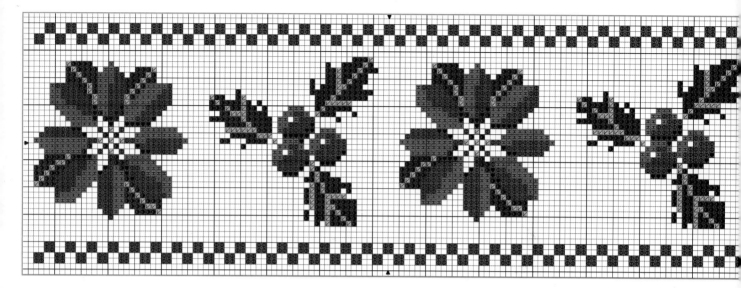

Materials

- White Aida band, (Zweigart E7316), 44 stitches wide and the same circumference as your cake, plus 1in (2.5cm)
- DMC stranded cotton threads as listed in the key
- Size 26 tapestry needle
- Cake

Design size

3⅛ x 9⅝in (7.7 x 24cm) at 14-count

Stitch count

44 x 134

	Thread key	DMC
I	Coral	351
◐	Red Bright	666
◪	Green	989
◑	Green Dark	986
▼	Red Dark	304

Note: use two strands for cross stitch

Method

1 Find the centre of the fabric and begin stitching from here following the chart. Work the cross stitches over one block of fabric.

2 Use three strands of thread as indicated in the key. There is no backstitch in this design.

3 Once you have completed the stitching, press the fabric, neaten the ends and wrap around the cake. Overlap the ends of the fabric and secure with double-sided sticky tape for easy removal. The cake band can be washed following the manufacturer's instructions.

Appendix

Suppliers and Sources of Information

Below is a list of suppliers who have kindly provided materials for the designs in this book, and a selection of other sources who can supply mail-order products for your own cross stitch designs. If you would like further information on good sources for cross stitch suppliers, there are many useful websites which can be accessed on the Internet.

UK

DMC Creative World Ltd.
Pullman Rd
Wigson
Leicester LE18 2DY
Tel: + 44 (0) 1162 811040
Website: www.dmc.com

Zweigart fabrics, DMC threads and accessories.

Framecraft
Lichfield Rd
Brownhills
Walsall
West Midlands WS8 6LH
Tel: + 44 (0) 1543 360842
Website: www.framecraft.com

Coasters, wooden boxes, ceramic bowls and a wide range of plastic items.

Fabric Flair
Warminster
Wiltshire BA12 0BG
Tel: + 44 (0) 1985 846400
Website: www.fabricflair.com

Extensive range of fabrics for cross stitch.

Impress
Slough Farm
Westhall
Halesworth
Suffolk IP19 8RN
Tel: + 44 (0) 1986 781422
Website www.impresscards.com

Cards, wooden boxes and other craft materials.

Card Art
14 Kensington Industrial Park
Hall Street
Southport
Merseyside PR9 0NY
Tel: + 44 (0) 1704 536040
Email: enq@cardart.co.uk

Corrugated paper, cards, craft items.

Debbie Cripps
8 Christchurch St. West
Frome
Somerset BA11 1EQ
Tel: + 44 (0) 1373 454448
Website: www.debbiecripps.co.uk

Doilies, novelty buttons and other items.

The Viking Loom
22 High Petergate
York YO1 7EH
Tel: + 44 (0) 1904 765599

Wooden boxes.

Craft Creations
Ingersall House
Delamare Road
Cheshunt
Hertfordshire EN8 9HD
Tel: + 44 (0) 1992 781900
Website: www.craftcreations.com

Three-fold cards and other craft items.

North America

Charles Craft
PO Box 1049
Laurinburg NC 28352
USA
Tel: (910) 844 3521
Fax: (910) 844 9846
Email: email@charlescraft.com

Fine line of cross stitch fabric and pre-finished accessories.

Crafter's Pride
PO Box 1105
Laurinburg NC 28353
USA
Tel: (910) 277 7441
Fax: (910) 277 837
Email: email@crafterspride.com

Provides top-quality cross stitch pre-finished accessories and designs. It also offers products by many less well-known cross stitch designers and suppliers.

About the Author

Joanne Sanderson worked for a number of years as a qualified Registered General Nurse. Her passion for cross stitch was inspired when asked by a friend to produce a design for her. A few months later, she entered and won a national competition to design a greetings card in cross stitch, which was a great inspiration. She decided to give up nursing and build on her passion for cross stitch by designing patterns full time. It was a very successful decision; her designs regularly feature in many popular cross stitch magazines, and she has recently been commissioned by DMC Creative World Ltd to design cross stitch kits.

In her spare time, Joanne's great passions are art, nature and gardening. She lives with her husband, daughter and two cats in South Yorkshire, England.

Acknowledgements

I would like to thank the following for helping to make this book possible:

Cara Ackerman at DMC Creative World Ltd, for all the threads and most of the fabrics used in this book; Lisa Reakes at Future Publishing for information on suppliers; Clare Hodgson at Future Publishing for her encouragement and support; and all the suppliers who kindly donated their products to finish and frame the designs.

A special thank you to my family for their understanding while I spent many long hours writing and stitching the designs for this book, especially my daughter Rianna who is a constant source of inspiration, and Alan for his support and encouragement. Thank you to my mother for all her support and love.

Finally, thank you to the Lord for all his blessings.

Index

Titles Available From
GMC PUBLICATIONS

Books

Woodcarving

Beginning Woodcarving	*GMC Publications*
Carving Architectural Detail in Wood: The Classical Tradition	*Frederick Wilbur*
Carving Birds & Beasts	*GMC Publications*
Carving the Human Figure: Studies in Wood and Stone	*Dick Onians*
Carving Nature: Wildlife Studies in Wood	*Frank Fox-Wilson*
Carving on Turning	*Chris Pye*
Celtic Carved Lovespoons: 30 Patterns	*Sharon Littley & Clive Griffin*
Decorative Woodcarving (New Edition)	*Jeremy Williams*
Elements of Woodcarving	*Chris Pye*
Essential Woodcarving Techniques	*Dick Onians*
Lettercarving in Wood: A Practical Course	*Chris Pye*
Making & Using Working Drawings for Realistic Model Animals	*Basil F. Fordham*
Power Tools for Woodcarving	*David Tippey*
Relief Carving in Wood: A Practical Introduction	*Chris Pye*
Understanding Woodcarving in the Round	*GMC Publications*
Woodcarving: A Foundation Course	*Zoë Gertner*
Woodcarving for Beginners	*GMC Publications*
Woodcarving Tools, Materials & Equipment (New Edition in 2 vols.)	*Chris Pye*

Woodturning

Adventures in Woodturning	*David Springett*
Bowl Turning Techniques Masterclass	*Tony Boase*
Chris Child's Projects for Woodturners	*Chris Child*
Colouring Techniques for Woodturners	*Jan Sanders*
Contemporary Turned Wood: New Perspectives in a Rich Tradition	*Ray Leier, Jan Peters & Kevin Wallace*
The Craftsman Woodturner	*Peter Child*
Decorating Turned Wood: The Maker's Eye	*Liz & Michael O'Donnell*
Decorative Techniques for Woodturners	*Hilary Bowen*
Green Woodwork	*Mike Abbott*
Illustrated Woodturning Techniques	*John Hunnex*
Intermediate Woodturning Projects	*GMC Publications*
Keith Rowley's Woodturning Projects	*Keith Rowley*
Making Screw Threads in Wood	*Fred Holder*
Turned Boxes: 50 Designs	*Chris Stott*
Turning Green Wood	*Michael O'Donnell*
Turning Pens and Pencils	*Kip Christensen & Rex Burningham*
Useful Woodturning Projects	*GMC Publications*
Woodturning: Bowls, Platters, Hollow Forms, Vases, Vessels, Bottles, Flasks, Tankards, Plates	*GMC Publications*
Woodturning: A Foundation Course (New Edition)	*Keith Rowley*
Woodturning: A Fresh Approach	*Robert Chapman*
Woodturning: An Individual Approach	*Dave Regester*
Woodturning: A Source Book of Shapes	*John Hunnex*
Woodturning Masterclass	*Tony Boase*
Woodturning Techniques	*GMC Publications*

Woodworking

Advanced Scrollsaw Projects	*GMC Publications*
Beginning Picture Marquetry	*Lawrence Threadgold*
Bird Boxes and Feeders for the Garden	*Dave Mackenzie*
Celtic Carved Lovespoons: 30 Patterns	*Sharon Littley & Clive Griffin*
Celtic Woodcraft	*Glenda Bennett*
Complete Woodfinishing (Revised Edition)	*Ian Hosker*
David Charlesworth's Furniture-Making Techniques	*David Charlesworth*
David Charlesworth's Furniture-Making Techniques – Volume 2	*David Charlesworth*
The Encyclopedia of Joint Making	*Terrie Noll*
Furniture-Making Projects for the Wood Craftsman	*GMC Publications*
Furniture-Making Techniques for the Wood Craftsman	*GMC Publications*
Furniture Projects with the Router	*Kevin Ley*
Furniture Restoration (Practical Crafts)	*Kevin Jan Bonner*
Furniture Restoration: A Professional at Work	*John Lloyd*
Furniture Restoration and Repair for Beginners	*Kevin Jan Bonner*
Furniture Restoration Workshop	*Kevin Jan Bonner*
Green Woodwork	*Mike Abbott*
Intarsia: 30 Patterns for the Scrollsaw	*John Everett*

Kevin Ley's Furniture Projects	*Kevin Ley*
Making Chairs and Tables	*GMC Publications*
Making Chairs and Tables – Volume 2	*GMC Publications*
Making Classic English Furniture	*Paul Richardson*
Making Heirloom Boxes	*Peter Lloyd*
Making Screw Threads in Wood	*Fred Holder*
Making Shaker Furniture	*Barry Jackson*
Making Woodwork Aids and Devices	*Robert Wearing*
Mastering the Router	*Ron Fox*
Pine Furniture Projects for the Home	*Dave Mackenzie*
Practical Scrollsaw Patterns	*John Everett*
Router Magic: Jigs, Fixtures and Tricks to Unleash your Router's Full Potential	*Bill Hylton*
Router Tips & Techniques	*Robert Wearing*
Routing: A Workshop Handbook	*Anthony Bailey*
Routing for Beginners	*Anthony Bailey*
Sharpening: The Complete Guide	*Jim Kingshott*
Sharpening Pocket Reference Book	*Jim Kingshott*
Simple Scrollsaw Projects	*GMC Publications*
Space-Saving Furniture Projects	*Dave Mackenzie*
Stickmaking: A Complete Course	*Andrew Jones & Clive George*
Stickmaking Handbook	*Andrew Jones & Clive George*
Storage Projects for the Router	*GMC Publications*
Test Reports: *The Router* and *Furniture & Cabinetmaking*	*GMC Publications*
Veneering: A Complete Course	*Ian Hosker*
Veneering Handbook	*Ian Hosker*
Woodfinishing Handbook (Practical Crafts)	*Ian Hosker*
Woodworking with the Router: Professional Router Techniques any Woodworker can Use	*Bill Hylton & Fred Matlack*

Toymaking

Scrollsaw Toy Projects	*Ivor Carlyle*
Scrollsaw Toys for All Ages	*Ivor Carlyle*

Dolls' Houses and Miniatures

1/12 Scale Character Figures for the Dolls' House	*James Carrington*
Americana in 1/12 Scale: 50 Authentic Projects	*Joanne Ogreenc & Mary Lou Santovec*
Architecture for Dolls' Houses	*Joyce Percival*
The Authentic Georgian Dolls' House	*Brian Long*
A Beginners' Guide to the Dolls' House Hobby	*Jean Nisbett*
Celtic, Medieval and Tudor Wall Hangings in 1/12 Scale Needlepoint	*Sandra Whitehead*
Creating Decorative Fabrics: Projects in 1/12 Scale	*Janet Storey*
The Dolls' House 1/24 Scale: A Complete Introduction	*Jean Nisbett*
Dolls' House Accessories, Fixtures and Fittings	*Andrea Barham*
Dolls' House Furniture: Easy-to-Make Projects in 1/12 Scale	*Freida Gray*
Dolls' House Makeovers	*Jean Nisbett*
Dolls' House Window Treatments	*Eve Harwood*
Easy to Make Dolls' House Accessories	*Andrea Barham*
Edwardian-Style Hand-Knitted Fashion for 1/12 Scale Dolls	*Yvonne Wakefield*
How to Make Your Dolls' House Special: Fresh Ideas for Decorating	*Beryl Armstrong*
Make Your Own Dolls' House Furniture	*Maurice Harper*
Making Dolls' House Furniture	*Patricia King*
Making Georgian Dolls' Houses	*Derek Rowbottom*
Making Miniature Chinese Rugs and Carpets	*Carol Phillipson*
Making Miniature Food and Market Stalls	*Angie Scarr*
Making Miniature Gardens	*Freida Gray*
Making Miniature Oriental Rugs & Carpets	*Meik & Ian McNaughton*
Making Period Dolls' House Accessories	*Andrea Barham*
Making Tudor Dolls' Houses	*Derek Rowbottom*
Making Victorian Dolls' House Furniture	*Patricia King*
Medieval and Tudor Needlecraft: Knights and Ladies in 1/12 Scale	*Sandra Whitehead*
Miniature Bobbin Lace	*Roz Snowden*
Miniature Embroidery for the Georgian Dolls' House	*Pamela Warner*
Miniature Embroidery for the Tudor and Stuart Dolls' House	*Pamela Warner*
Miniature Embroidery for the Victorian Dolls' House	*Pamela Warner*

Crafts

Gardening

Photography

Art Techniques

Magazines

Woodturning ◆ Woodcarving ◆ Furniture & Cabinetmaking ◆ New Woodworking

The Router ◆ The Dolls' House Magazine ◆ Black & White Photography

Outdoor Photography ◆ Travel Photography ◆ Machine Knitting News ◆ BusinessMatters

The above represents a full list of all titles currently published or scheduled to be published. All are available direct from the Publishers or through bookshops, newsagents and specialist retailers. To place an order, or to obtain a complete catalogue, contact:

GMC Publications,

Castle Place, 166 High Street, Lewes, East Sussex BN7 1XU, United Kingdom
Tel: 01273 488005   Fax: 01273 478606   E-mail: pubs@thegmcgroup.com
ORDERS BY CREDIT CARD ARE ACCEPTED